Understanding History

Dr. Adil Firdous Wani

PRABHAKAR PRAKASHAN

Hardcover ISBN: 978-93-67002-47-6
Paperback ISBN: 978-93-67003-44-2
eBook ISBN: 978-93-67002-31-5

© **Author**

Prabhakar Prakashan (P) Ltd.
Plot No.-55, Main Mother Dairy Road
Pandav Nagar, East Delhi-110092
Phone: 011-40395855
WhatsApp: +91 8368220032
E-mail: sales@pharosbooks.in
Website: www.prabhakarprakashan.com
First Edition: 2023

UNDERSTANDING HISTORY
Dr. Adil Firdous Wani

This book has been written on the basis of deep study and other available written records of ancient and Modern India, using different sources to servestudents fraternity and Research Scholars with the best of my knowledge andresources. This book provides valuable information regarding Ancient India and Modern India.

Dr. Adil Firdous Wani

Dedication

This book is dedicated to my parents who showed me this world and made me aware of my existence, because what I am today would not have been possible without their blessing.

UNDERSTANDING HISTORY

Indian History: Indigenous Vision

'Understanding History' is an honest academic effort to identify the soul of India. To recognize that soul which was forgotten somewhere in the overcast of colonial knowledge exchanged. This book is a serious attempt to write, understand and present Indian history in its original form. In other words, this book creates a base of knowledge and history.

Starting with the concept of 'Bharatvarsha', this book in its study goes through different phases, stages and periods of history from Ancient India to its seriousness. While examining them objectively, the renaissance, understanding the different dimensions of the freedom movement, bringing them to the fore, brings us to the present situation of India. Certainly, the one thing that is worth noting the most in this whole process is the author's indigenous vision of historiography, which does not allow that subtle insight to disappear even for a moment anywhere in its own investigation. Understanding India's long history from a new point of view, especially from the point of view of historical account with indigenous modernity is a laborious and patient work. It is heartening to see that today's youth, understanding the politics of knowledge of the colonial period properly, also have a proper constructive response to it. They understanding it properly that the colonial enlightenment does not consider our traditional indigenous knowledge as knowledge at all. Considered it in the category of superstition. But when this book conveys Indian contribution in the field of medicine to the world through Charak, Sushruta, then by way of revealing the politics of the concept of colonial knowledge, it also brings its hollowness and exploitative form in front of us. India, which brought forth the concept of devotion following the 'Vedas' and 'Puranas', is today moving step by step with the world of science and technology. Understanding the concept of 'Swadeshi' and 'Swaraj', this book seriously considers the 'self-reliant India' concept, 'Jan Dhan' accounts as well as many other public welfare government schemes of the present.

This whole book actually underlines in its concept that in the centre of the entire concept of Indian knowledge tradition and thinking, the welfare of the people or the common man or the living beings is included. This is the reason why when Gandhi Ji talks about the last man, then Indian culture in its entirety proclaims 'Vasudhev Kutumbakam' and 'Satyamev Jayate'. The most important thing is that being associated with tradition and culture, being proud of it, does not mean being old-fashioned. Taking pride in Indian culture and history, being connected to it, we are rapidly moving towards 'Self-reliant India' through 'Digital India'. Indian history is testimony to the fact that innovation has been welcomed.

I have full hope that this book will generate interest in Indian history among students and researchers. This book makes a meaningful intervention in Indian history writing and traditional knowledge and fills an academic gap.

Siddharth Chaturvedi

CONTENTS

1.1 BHARATAVARSHA: CONCEPT & EVOLUTION- VEDIC, EPIC & PURANIC TRADITIONS AND MAKING OF MODERN INDIA

BASIC INFORMATION ABOUT INDIA OR BHARATVARSHA

India is the seventh largest country by area and second largest by population and also the most populous country in the world.

Name: The Republic of India

Capital: New Delhi

Continent: Asia

Location: 28°36.8′N, 77°12.5′E

Other Names of India: Hindustan/Bharat

Indian States: 28

Union Territories: 8

Neighbour countries: China, Nepal, Bangladesh, Sri Lanka, Pakistan, Myanmar, Bhutan, Afghanistan, Maldives

Official Languages: Hindi and English

Independence: 15th August 1947

Head of country: President

Head of government: Prime Minister

Apex judicial body: Supreme Court

Currency: Indian Rupee

National Flag: Tricolour

National Emblem: Lion of Sarnath

National Anthem: Jana Gana Mana

National Song: Vande Mataram

National Animal: Tiger

National Flower: Lotus

National Calendar: Saka calendar

National Tree: Banyan

National Bird: Peacock

National Day:

- 26th January- Republic Day
- 15th August- Independence Day
- 2nd October- Gandhi Jayanti

Population: 1,342,512,706

Area: 3.287 million km²

Total Coast Line of India: 7,517 km

Land Frontier: 15,200 km

Stretch: 2933 km East to West, 3214 km North to South

Important Rivers: Ganges, Brahmaputra, Indus, Godavari, Mahanadi, Krishna, Kaveri,Luni, Narmada, Yamuna, Sutlej, Jhelum

Important Mountains: Himalaya, Eastern Ghats, Western Ghats, Karakoram, Aravalli, Satpura

Highest point: Kanchenjunga

Seas: Bay of Bengal, Arabian Sea, Indian Ocean

Major agricultural climates: Kharif, Rabi, Zaid

Major Cities: Mumbai, Kolkata, New Delhi, Bangalore, Chennai, Ahmedabad, Pune, Hyderabad, Surat, Indore, Jaipur, Kanpur, Lucknow, Vadodara, Kochi.

BHARATVARSHA CONCEPT AND EVOLUTION

Bharatvarsha: Bharatavarsha is named after emperor Bharata, the son of Shakuntala and Dushyanta who conquered the Indian sub-continent where people lived in peace and harmony. Bharata Varsha is the ancient name of India. It means the land of the people who belonged to the Bharata clan. Bharatvarsha is even mentioned in Puranas. According to Vishnu Purana, it is mentioned as, "The country that lies north of the ocean and south of the snowy mountains is called Bharata Varsha".

India is a country in south Asia whose name is derived from the river Indus (Sindhu) The name Bharat is used as a designation for the country in our constitution. India is the seventh largest country in the world in terms of area and the second most populous country in the world in terms of population. India shares the longest boundary with Bangladesh and the smallest boundary with Afghanistan followed by China, Pakistan, Nepal, Myanmar and Bhutan. In the south on the eastern side, the Gulf of Mannar and Palk Strait separate India from Sri Lanka.

* **Vedic Concept:** In the seventh mandala (chapter) of the Rigveda, the Battle of ten kings has been described as Dasha Rajana war. This war was fought between ten powerful tribes and Sudasa, the king of the Bharata tribe. Sudasa defeated all of them on the bank of river Ravi (Purushni/Iravati). After victory Sudasa gained popularity among the masses and people started identifying themselves as members of the Bharata tribe. The name Bharata stuck to people's lips and with the time came to be called "Bharata Varsha" meaning the land of Bharata.

Idea Of Bharatvarsham: Bharatvarsha stands for the country India which is mentioned by different names since ancient times. The Country is named after an emperor Bharat. According to sources and some tales he was the son of Shakuntala and Dushyanta and the country is named after him "Bharata Varsha" which means the Land of Bharat. Puranas also define the country i.e. India as Bharatvarsha.

*** Puranic Concept:** In Vishnu Purana, it is described as "The country (Varsham) that lies north of the ocean and south of snowy mountains is called Bharatvarsham."

Vishnu Purana also explains the naming of the country. Bharat came much later in the chronology, and he ruled one of the kingdoms under Bharat Varsha (Modern day equivalent to India. Bharat, the great king, expanded his kingdom to the oceans. This part of the land was then called Bharat Varsha (even when we had independent kingdoms in Kashi, Magadha, Anga, Kuru, Kaushala, Vaideha and Kalinga).

In traditional and legendary Hindu literature, India is called Bharatakhanda. The present name of India is derived from river Sindhu (The Indus). Many historians and scholars have given their different views regarding how the name Bharatvarsh had been derived. According to the Aitareya Brahmana "Bharata was a universal monarch who had built a vast empire and had ruled over vast areas of land in all the four directions". It is said that the Monarch had performed Aswamedha Yajna to assert his supremacy over the weaker ones. The foreigners have referred to the entire country from the Himalayas to Kanyakumari as India. The Muslim rulers called the country Hindustan. The British rulers called the country India. It means that India has three names. India, Hindustan, and Bharat. Bharat is short of Bharatvarsham. According to ancient writings known as the Puranas, Bharata concurred the whole subcontinent of India and ruled the land in peace and harmony. In this content, it could be said that the name Bharatvarsha had been derived from the "Bharata"

                    UNDERSTANDING HISTORY

race of Vedic Aryans because this race is known to be at the forefront of contemporary political power. The Bharatas were a venerable and Ancient tribe which is mentioned in Rig Veda, specifically in Mandala III of Bharata Rishi Vishwamitra, as well as in other ancient texts. Mandala VII states that the Bharatas were victorious in the Battle of the ten Kings. This is supported by historical evidence.

According to the Aitareya Brahmana, "Bharata was a universal monarch who had built a vast empire winning vast areas of land which spreads all over the four directions".

EPICS

Epics: Epics are longer poems derived from the oral tradition which narrates the deeds and adventures of heroic or legendary figures and the past history of India.

- **Mahabharata**
- **Ramayana**
- **Panchtantra**
- **Puranas**

1. **Mahabharata:** Mahabharata was written by Veda Vyas. It has one lakh and ten thousand couplets in 18 sections. It is the longest epic of India and the world's largest epic. It also contains the famous Bhagavad Gita.

2. **Ramayana:** Ramayana is an ancient Sanskrit text. Ramayana was written by Valmiki. Ramayana is the story of Lord Rama. It tells us about Lord Rama. It has 96,000 verses.

3. **Panchtantra:** It was written by Vishnu Sharma. It is a renowned collection of short stories. It is an ancient Sanskrit text.

From Ramayana,we gather some historical facts:

- There was a struggle between Aryans and Non Aryans.

- During the Vedic Period, the power of the king had increased and he performed Ashvamedha sacrifice to assert his political supremacy over the states.

- During the Vedic Period the position of women declined.

- Ramayana also indicates the expansion of Aryans towards the south.

PURANAS

Puranas: Puranas are more or less real histories of ancient India. Puranas are 18 in number.

Some important ones are:

- Vayu Purana

- Vishnu Purana

- Skanda Purana

- Brahma Purana

1. **Vayu Purana:** Vayu Purana is the oldest Purana. The surviving manuscripts of Vayu Purana have about 12,000 verses.

2. **Vishnu Purana:** It is the important Panchatantra text in the Vaishnavism literature corpus. It has about 7,000 verses.

3. **Skanda Purana:** The Skanda Purana contains over 81,000 verses and is of Kaumara literature titled after Skanda, a son of Shiva and Parvati, who is also known as Murugan.

Apart from providing political perspectives, Hemchandra Raychaudhuri attempted a spatial/territorial explanation of the ancient Bharatavarsha and in course of it, engaged extensively with Puranic literature.[1]

Importance of Puranas:

- Puranas contain the genealogical and dynastic chronology of kings. Each king has been mentioned in his reigning period.

- Puranas help us to know the historical geography of India.

- Puranas tell us about the achievements of kings and even throw light on the social, economic and religious milieu of India.

1.2. STATE AND IMPERIAL FORMATION: RISE OF JANAPADAS, THE MAURYAS, THE KUSHANS, THE GUPTAS, THE PALLAVAS, THE CHOLAS AND THE VIJAYANAGARA EMPIRE.

RISE OF JANAPADAS

Meaning of Janapada: Janapada is a Sanskrit term which is composed of two words i.e.. 'Jana' and 'Pada' Jana means 'people' or 'subject' and Pada means 'foot'. It means the land where the Jana or people set their feet and settled down at a place is called Janapada. The Janapadas were the major kingdoms of the Vedic period.

During the Vedic period, the family or Kula was the basic unit of political organization which was headed by the head of the family known as Kulapati or Grihapati. The next unit was village. Village was known as Grama which was headed by the Gramini. Many villages formed a Vis or group which was headed by the Vishapati. The highest unit was Jana or tribe i.e.. a group of Vis which was headed by the tribal chief. The tribal chief was called Rajan (the king).

In the later Vedic period, these tribal organizations changed their identity from tribes to territorial area and these areas were called Janapadas or states. It was during the 6th century B.C. onwards that the use of iron started in the Gangetic plain which created the conditions for the formation of large territorial states. It was only because of such developments that these Janapadas became more powerful and finally turned into larger states called Mahajanapadas.

There were 16 Mahajanapadas during 600 B.C. mentioned in Buddhist literature (Anguttara Nikaya) and in Jain literature

(Bhagvatisutta). Out of these 16 Mahajanapadas, the kingdom of Magadh emerged as the most powerful Kingdom.

Nature of 16 Mahajanapadas:

Mahajanapadas literally means the "great realm".

- Monarchical Mahajanapada: There existed a Monarchical form of govt. It means the king was the head of the territory. The king performed various sacrifices. One such sacrifice was called the Ashvamedha sacrifice.

- Republican Mahajanapada: It means that form of government. where the supreme power rescales in a body of citizens. It means the king was elected from a group of people. There is a reference to two popular assemblies or institutions. i.e.. 'sabha' and 'samiti'.

- Sabha was the selected body of elders. The Sabha advised the king on administration. It also functioned as a court of law and even tried cases dealing with crimes. The head of the Sabha was called 'Sabhapati'.

- The Samiti was the most popular assembly which included all common people as a part of it. The main function of the samiti was to elect and re-elect the king (Rajan). The head of the Samiti was called 'Pati'.

Rise of Magadha: Magadh emerged as the most powerful kingdom. Three dynasties namely the Haryanka dynasty, Shishunaga dynasty and Nanda dynasty ruled in Magadha at different times.

The four Mahajanapadas Magadha, Kosala, Avanti and Vatsa fought for supremacy from the 6th century B.C. to the 4th century B.C. At last, Magadha emerged victorious. It emerged as the most powerful state in ancient India. Magadha is situated in Bihar. It is said that Jarasandha, a descendant of Brihadratha formed this empire in Magadha.The most powerful dynasty in Magadha was the Haryanka dynasty which rose to

                    UNDERSTANDING HISTORY

prominence under Bimbisara who was the first ruler and the founder of this dynasty which ruled from 558 B.C. to 491 B.C. He ruled for 52 years. He was a contemporary and follower of Gautam Buddha. He ruled from his capital Girivraj/Rajagriha. Bimbisara was also known as "Sreniya". He is said to be the first king who had a standing army and it was only under his rule that Magadha came into prominence. In order to strengthen his political position, he entered into matrimonial alliances. He followed the policy of conquests and expansion. He had an excellent system of administration.

Bimbisara was succeeded by his son, Ajatshatru who ruled from 492 B.C. to 460 B.C. His mother's name was Chellana. It is said that Ajatshatru in order to assume the powers killed his father Bimbisara and himself became the ruler. He embraced Buddhism. The first Buddhist Council was convened by him at Rajagriha in 483 B.C. after the death of Gautam Buddha under the chairmanship of Mahakashyap. Ajatshatru was succeeded by his son Udayin who ruled from 460 B.C. to 444 B.C. He shifted the capital from Rajagriha to Patliputra. His reign is important because he built the fort upon the confluence of Ganga and son at Pataliputra. Udayin was succeeded by Shisunaga who killed his own king i.e. Nagadasak and himself became the ruler and thus laid the foundation of a new dynasty known as Shisunaga Dynasty. After assuming the powers,he temporarily shifted the capital from Patliputra to Vaishali. The most important achievement of Shishunaga was the destruction of Avanti with its capital at Ujjain and this brought an end to the 100 years old rivalry between Magadha and Avanti.

Avanti then became a fort of Magadha. After Shisunagas, came the Nandas whose first ruler was Mahapadma Nanda. He is rightly called the first historical emperor of India. The last ruler of the Nanda Dynasty was Dhanananda. He was defeated by Chandragupta Maurya with the assistance of Kautilya (Chanakya) and in this way laid the foundation of a new dynasty known as the Mauryan dynasty.

MAURYAN EMPIRE

Chronology of Mauryan Rulers:

Chandragupta Maurya -321 to 297 B.C. (Jainism religion)

Bindusara -297 to 272 B.C.

Ashoka- 272 to 232 B.C.

Dashratha - 252 to 224 B.C.

Samprati -224 to 215 B.C.

Salisuka - 215 to 202 B.C.

Devavarman - 202 to195 B.C.

Satadhanvan -195 to 187 B.C.

Brihadratha -187 to 185 B.C.

The last ruler of the Mauryan Empire was Brihadratha who was defeated by his own Commander-in-chief i.e. Pushyamitra Sunga who then founded the Sunga dynasty.

Introduction: The Mauryan empire covered most part of the Indian subcontinent from the end of the 4th century to the beginning of the 2nd century. Chandragupta Maurya was the founder of this dynasty who had ruled from the Magadha. A new chapter in the cultural and political history of India begins with the advent of the Mauryas. The Mauryas gave political unity to India. Mauryan Dynasty is considered the first historical dynasty of India. Dr. V.A Smith has pointed out, "With the establishment of Mauryan Dynasty, the history of ancient India emerges from darkness to light."

The foundation of the Mauryan Empire in 321 B.C. by Chandragupta Maurya was a unique event in the history of India. Mauryan Empire originated from the kingdom of Magadha. In the Indo-Gangatic plains, there are many sources which help us to reconstruct the history of Mauryas.

Chandragupta Maurya (324/321 – 297 BCE), the founder of the Mauryan dynasty, received a strong army from the Nandas, which he used to conquer virtually all of north India, the north-west, and a significant section of peninsular India[2].

According to various historical sources, Chandragupta Maurya was the first ruler of this Dynasty. He became the ruler with the advice and guidance of Kautilya or Chanakya, a Brahmin advisor who was the author of the great ancient Indian treatise on politics and economy i.e. Arthashastra.

Chandragupta Maurya's successor Bindusara improved trade relations with neighbouring kingdoms. He also entered into marriage alliances with other kingdoms end annexed them. He was succeeded by his son, Ashoka who became an active exponent of peace and stupas, monasteries and other religious buildings were also constructed during Ashoka's reign.

Ashoka and Kalinga War: The Mauryan empire reached its peak during the time of Ashoka, the son of Bindusara and the Grandson of Chandra Gupta Maurya. The conquest of Kalinga in 261 B.C. (fought in modern Odisha) in the eighteenth year of his reign brought about a great revolution in the life of Ashoka and after this war he changed his path and followed the principles of Dharma. After this bloodshed war, he abandoned conquering the territories and began to work for the welfare of his people as he had embraced Buddhism after this war. The miseries, sufferings, sorrows, and destructions which were the outcome of the Kalinga war changed his heart as he now realized the pain of his people. He thereafter made a declaration that "From this time onwards there will be no beating of war drums but the drums of Dharma will be beaten. There will be no conquests of territories, but the conquest of Dharma will be made."[3]

This is the only major war which was fought by Ashoka after his accession to the throne. In fact, this war marks the close of empire buildings and military conquests of ancient India that began with the Mauryan Emperor Chandragupta Maurya. No war is as important either for its intensity or its results as the Kalinga war of Ashoka. It is said that this war changed the heart of the victory from cruelty to that of piety. The war was completed in the 8th year of Ashoka's accession to the throne probably in 261 B.C. After this bloodshed battle for the throne. He took a pledge to never again wage such a war of conquest.

(In the Kalinga war about 1,00,000 people were killed and about 1,50,000 people were taken captive).

SOURCES OF HISTORY:

A. Literary Sources: Literary sources, are all written records in the form of texts, essays or descriptions, manuscripts, epics etc.

1. **Puranas:** From Puranas we came to know that Chandragupta Maurya belonged to the Shudra caste.

2. **Jain Traditions:** That Mauryas were knwon as Moriyas during that time i.e. they belong to a region where there were many peacocks.

3. **Buddhist Texts:** From Buddhist texts i.e. Dighanakya, Mahavasma and Divyavadana, We came to know that Mauryas belonged to a Kshatriya clan of Moriyas and later came to be known as Mauryas.

4. **Parisisthaparvana:** Parisishtparvana written by Hemachandra, tells us that Chandragupta Maurya, the first powerful king of India was the son of the daughter of a chief of a village who tamed peacocks or one who was the rearer of peacocks (Mayura Poshaka).

5. **Mudrarakshasa:** From Mudrarakshasa written by Vishakdhatta, we came to know that Mauryas were of low origin. The historical drama in Sanskrit "Signet Ring of the Rakshasa, the chief minister of the last Nanda monarch" by Vishakhadatta (4th

   UNDERSTANDING HISTORY

century CE) describes the ascension of the king Chandragupta Maurya to power in Northern India with the assistance of Chanakya, his Guru and chief minister.[4]

6. **Arthashastra:** Chanakya, the political advisor of Chandragupta Maurya authored 'Arthashastra'. Arthashastra is a treatise on state craft, economic policy and military strategy, written in Sanskrit. Arthashastra gives detailed information regarding the Mauryas.

7. **Indica:** 'Indica' authored by Greek traveller and historian Megasthnese gives detailed information on the social, economic and administrative condition of the Mauryan empire.

B. Epigraphy: Epigraphy is the science of identifying graphics, classifying their uses according to dates and cultural contents and drawing conclusions about the writing and the writers. So, these pieces of evidence are the ones identified on inscriptions, clay tablets etc.

C. Archaeological sources: Archaeological sources are basically material evidence like historical buildings and other remains that give important and detailed information pertaining to a particular period.

Inscriptions are basically, scriptures and drawings on Monoliths, stones and relatively on hard materials and act as an important source for history as they tell us about aspects varying from messages, ownership of property, victories over other kingdoms, humans, shlokas, stories of the movements, praises on the king and much more to add on to the list.

Inscriptions are mainly found in:

- Rock edicts
- Pillar inscriptions
- Written records

The main language of inscriptions are Prakrit, Pali, and Sanskrit.

The inscriptions on the major rock edicts are as follows:

- Declares prohibition of animal sacrifice; also prohibits the holding of festivals; royal hunting was discontinued; only 2 peacocks and deer were killed in the kitchen of beloved of Gods.

- It mentions the medical treatment of humans and animals. It also mentions the construction of roads, wells etc and also tree planting.

- It mentions the Pradeshikas, Rajukkas and Yuktas; declares liberty towards Brahmas and the Sramanas.

- It mentions that the Beri Ghosa has been replaced by Dharma Gosha. It also mentions that the Rajukas had the power to punish.

- Reference to the appointment of Dhamma Mahatmas for the first time in the 14th year of his reign. It also mentions Dhamma Mahatmas promoting the welfare of prisoners.

- King considered the victory by Dhamma to be the foremost victory; mention the Dhamma victory on the Greeks being named Antiochus. It also mentions the Dhamma victory.

- **Administration of the Mauryas:** The Mauryas organised a huge administrative system. Chandragupta Maurya was not only a powerful ruler but also a capable administrator.

1. **Central Administration:**
- **King:** The king was the head of the state. He had all the powers. There were no references to any election of the king in records. Usually the eldest son succeeded to the throne.
- **Ministers:** Next to the king, ministers occupied an important place in politics. The council of ministers is called Parishad. According to Kautilya "A single wheel can never move, hence he shall employ ministers and hear their opinion."

2. **District Administration:** Each district was administrated by some officers like Pradeshika, Yukta and Rajukka. Pradeshika was the senior and Rajukka was subordinate to him. Yukta was subordinate to both of them. It was the duty of Pradeshika to favour the kingdom every five years.

3. **Village Administration:** The village was the smallest unit of administration. Its head was known as Gramika. He was not a paid servant of the crown but an elected official of the village.

4. **Municipal Administration:** Magasthenes gives an elaborate description of the administration of Patliputra and it is assumed that other important towns were governed in a similar way. According to him, towns were controlled by a Municipal commission of 30 members who were divided into 6 boards of 5 members each.

5. **Judicial Administration:** The Mauryan state had a very efficient and well managed judicial system. The king was the head of justice. There were two classes of court i.e. 'Dharmasthiya' (civil courts) and 'Kantakshodan' (criminal courts).

6. **Military Organisation:** The Mauryas maintained a large and well-equipped army which was three times larger than the Nandas. The fighting force of the Mauryan government consisted of 60,000 infantry, 30,000 cavalry and 9000 elephants. Senapati was the head of this Military department.

Conclusion: In the end, we can say that Chandragupta Maurya successfully overthrew Dhanananda,the last ruler of Nanda dynasty. The Mauryan kings ruled almost the entire sub-continent. The Mauryan period is considered to be the greatest since the kingdom grew into a powerful one and also excelled in administrative reforms.

KUSHAN EMPIRE

KUSHANS:

Chronology: Kujula Kadphises: (30-80 C.E.)

Vima Kadphises: (95-127 C.E.)

Kanishka: (127-150 A.D.)

It is believed that Kushanas belong to the nomadic race of the Yu-Chi tribe (Central Asian tribe). Kushanas are also known as Tokarians or Tochanians. They first captured Bactria, an ancient country lying between the north of Hindukush mountains and the Oxus river (Amu Darya river) now a part of Afghanistan, Tajikistan and Uzbekistan. The first ruler of Kushana dynasty was Kujula Kadphises.[5]

He ousted Shakas from Bactria and his empire extended from the river Oxus to the river Indus. He was the first ruler among the Kushanas who issued copper coins. He assumed various titles like Maharajadhiraja, Maharaja Mahant and also styled himself as Maharajadharmasthaya. The court language of Kushanas was 'Sanskrit'. All their inscriptions are also in the Sanskrit language. Kujula Kadphises was succeeded by his own son Vima Kadphises or Kadphises II. He is also known as Wemo in his Greek coins. He conquered India and extended his control over the region east of the Indus. He issued gold coins and his coins contained pictures of Lord Shiva. From these coins we also came to know that he was a worshipper of Lord Shiva. He was defeated by Chinese General Panchao and was compelled to pay annual tributes.

The sources of the Kushanas period are scanty. The coins of the Kushan kings help us to know the history of the Kushan dynasty. The coins of the Kadphises I and Kadphises II tell us that Kushans ruled over a vast empire. The figures of Shiva are engraved on the coins of Kadphises II on the basis of which it can be said that he was the worshipper/devotee of Lord Shiva and that he had commercial relations with countries abroad and that is also revealed by the study of these coins. Besides coins, we have some literary sources like 'Buddhacharitra' by 'Ashvaghosa', which throws a flood of light on the events connected with Kanishka. No material has so far been discovered to know the history of Kushans after Kadphises II and prior to Kanishka. Even this cannot be said with certainty whether Kanishka was related to Kadphises II or not.[6]

KANISHKA:

Reign: 2nd century (127–150 A.D.)

Predecessor: Vima Kadphises

Successor: Huvishka

Born: Possibly Khotan, present-day Xinjiang, China (per Chinese chronicles) or Kashmir

Dynasty: Kushan

Religion: Buddhism

Kanishka was an emperor of the Kushan dynasty. He ruled from 127–150 C.E. It was during his reign that the Kushan empire reached its zenith. He is famous for his military, political, and spiritual achievements.

The exact relationship between Wima Kadphises or Kadphises II and Kanishka is not clear. Kanishka is regarded as the famous ruler of the Kushans dynasty. His reign is famous for two things:

1. He started the SAKA ERA which commenced in 78 A.D.

2. He gave full patronage to Mahayana Buddhism.

Kanishka is regarded as the 'Second Ashoka' on account of his contribution to Mahayana Buddhism. He conquered Kashmir and founded a town there, i.e. Kanishkpura. He is said to have defeated the Saka Satrapas of Punjab and Mathura. He then invaded and annexed Magadha. It is said that a Lichchavi ruler of Magadha presented 'Ashvagosh' a famous Buddhist scholar to Kanishka.

Traditions stated that Kanishka is said to be killed by his own generals as they were tired of his almost continuous expeditions. He ruled from two capitals, one was at Purushpura and the second was at Mathura. He convened the fourth Buddhist council in 72 A.D. at Kundalvan (Kashmir) under the chairmanship of Vasumitra and the vice chairmanship of Ashvagosa. The proceedings were written and compiled in a book called "Mahavibhasa". This book is called as the 'Encyclopaedia of Buddhism' written in the Sanskrit language. The court language of the Kushans was Sanskrit. All their inscriptions which have been found as a part of their evidence are in the Sanskrit language also. Kanishka is said to have constructed a wooden tower in Purushpura which was even mentioned by Huien-Tsang (a Chinese traveller) and Alberuni (an Arab traveller).[7]

GUPTA DYNASTY

Guptas Chronology:

After the fall of the Kushanas, Guptas came to power.

Sri Gupta - 240-280 A.D.

Ghatotkach Gupta -280-320 A.D.

Chandra Gupta I -320-335 A.D.

Samudra Gupta -335-375 A.D.

Rama Gupta -375-380 A.D.

Chandra Gupta II- 380-413 A.D.

Kumara Gupta -413-455 A.D.

Skandha Gupta - 455-468 A.D.

Later Guptas were: Purana Gupta, Narsimha Gupta, Kumar Gupta II, Brahma Gupta and Vishnu Gupta.

GUPTAS: After the fall of the Kushanas, the Guptas came to power. Guptas gave a new shape and political unity to India. It was during this time that India made rapid progress. Samudra Gupta and Chandragupta II were not only great conquerors but also brave commanders and great administrators. Sri Gupta was the founder of this dynasty and assumed the title of Maharaja.[8]

Sources of the Gupta Empire

There are many sources which help us to reconstruct the history of the Guptas:

- Literary sources
- Archaeological sources &
- Foreign sources

A. Literary sources:

(i) Puranas:

"Anu Ganga Prayagam Cha Saketam Magadham Statha

Etan Janapadan Servan Bhakshyante Gupta Vamsajah"

This reference indicate that, "along the Gangas, all the territories of Prayaga, Magadha and Sāketa will be enjoyed by the Gupta family." However, it does not give us the information that which king ruled on which territory but it certainly indicates that the empire of the Guptas included these states.

(ii) Kamaudi Mahautsav: Among the literary source next to Puranas is Kamaudi Mahaustav. It is from this source that we learn that there was a king of Magadha, whose name was Sundervarman, He adopted a son namely Chandrasena who formed a military alliance with Lichchavis and killed his father and he himself became the ruler of Magadha.

Dr. K.P. Jayswal has identified Chandrasena with Chandragupta. The identification cannot be accepted historically. Chandragupta according to certain writers cannot be identified with Chandrasena. Moreover, Chandragupta had not sought a military alliance with the Lichchavis but only entered into a matrimonial alliance.

(iii) Devi Chandraguptam: Another important play is Devi Chandraguptam. It is from this source that we came to know that Samudra Gupta was succeeded by his son Rama Gupta. He had to wage a war against the Saka king. During this war, he was put in such a precarious position that in order to save his life and kingdom agreed to surrender his wife Dhruva Devi. This was an act that his younger brother Chandragupta II could not tolerate. So he himself decided to go to the Saka king in the disguise of Dhruva Devi. The strategy succeeded. Chandragupta II killed the Saka king. This elevated the prestige and personality of Chandragupta II not only in the eyes of the people but also in the eyes of Dhruva Devi. Ramagupta could not tolerate that and then he made the plan of killing his own brother Chandragupta II. But before he could do that Chandragupta II killed his own brother Rama Gupta and married the widow of his brother.

(iv) Bana Bhatta's Harish Charitra: Though Harishchandra was reduced to writing at a very late stage, yet it throws light on the relationship of later Gupta kings with the kings of the Vardhana dynasty.

(v) Arya Maurya Sri Mulakalpa: It is a Buddhist chronicle which helps us to know the history of eastern, western, northern and southern dynasties.

(vi) Kamandak's Nitishastra: Kamandak was a disciple of Vishnu Gupta or Chanakya. His "Nitishastra" help us to know about Gupta's polity.

B. Archaeological sources:

1. **Coins:** The study of coins is called Numismatics. Almost all the Gupta kings issued their own coins. These coins have proved very useful for the reconstruction of the history of the Guptas. It is from these coins we learn the names and titles of the kings. Samudra Gupta had assumed the title of 'Param Bhattarka'. Further these coins also help us to know about the economic condition of the Guptas. These coins also throw light on the religious condition and personal religion of Gupta kings. Most of the coins of Samudra Gupta and Chandra Gupta on their reverse bear the images of Goddess Lakshmi.

2. **Allahabad Pillar Inscription:** This is also known as Allahabad Pillar Prasasti. It was composed by Harisena. This inscription consists of 33 lines without any commas or full stops. This inscription highlights the achievement of Samudra Gupta, his conquests of north & South India and his relations with border tribes & states. In short, without this inscription the history of Samudra Gupta would have been incomplete.

3. **Eran stone pillar inscription:** Another important inscription of this period is Eran Stone Pillar Inscription. It helps us to construct the history of Chandragupta II.

4. **Mehrauli Iron pillar inscription:** This inscription describe the achievements of a king called Chandra. However, there are a lot of controversies regarding his identification and that is still undecided.

5. **Bhitari Pillar inscriptions:** This inscription provides us information about the fratricidal conflict most probably between Skanda Gupta and other claimants to the throne.

Monuments are the other important source regarding the history of the Guptas. Most famous among these were the schools of arts at Banaras & Nalanda. Beside the painting of Ajanta and Ellora caves throws a flood of life on Indian culture. These monuments and painting helps us in the reconstruction of social and religious history of the Guptas.

C. Foreign Sources:

Other important sources from which we get information about the Guptas are foreign sources. India, the land of Gautam Buddha from time to time attracted various foreigners from different countries.

During the Gupta period Fahein visited India during the reign of Chandragupta II. He started from China in 339 A.D. and reached India in 414 A.D. He stayed in Patliputra for a period of 3 years. His accounts expound on the political, social, economic and religious condition of the Guptas under Chandragupta II.

PALLAVA DYNASTY

Capital: Kanchipuram

Common languages: Prakrit, Sanskrit, Tamil

Religion: Hinduism, Jainism, Buddhism

Government: Monarchy

- **Established: 275 C.E.**
- **Destablished: 897 C.E.**

Preceded by: Kalabhra dynasty and Satavahana dynasty

Succeeded by: Chola dynasty, Kadamba dynasty and Western Ganga dynasty

Geographical location today: Sri Lanka

The Pallavas: The Pallava Dynasty ruled in the south Indian subcontinent. The span of pallava's reign was from 275 C.E. to 897 C.E. The capital from where they ruled was Kanchipuram. They were the most influential rulers of south India and contributed enormously to the fields of religion, philosophy, art, coins, and architecture. Pallavas became a major south Indian power during the reign of Mahendravarman I and Narsimhavarman I. Throughout their rule in Tondaimandalam, they were in constant conflict with both Chalukayas of Badami in the north and the Tamil kingdom of Cholas and Pandyas in the south. They are most remembered for their share temple architecture.[9]

Political History of Pallavas:

- The Pallavas' origin is shrouded in mystery. Historians have proposed several theories.

- According to some historians, they are a branch of the Parthain people (an Iranian tribe) who gradually migrated to south-India.

- Some claim that they are an indigenous dynasty that arose in the southern region and was a mix of various tribe.

- Some experts believe that they are of Naga origin and first settled near Madras in the Tondaimandalam region.

- Another theory holds they are the offspring of a Chola prince and a Naga princess from Manivallam (Sri Lanka).

- Other believed that Pallavas were feudatories of Satavanhenas.

- The first Pallava kings ruled in the early fourth century A.D.

- By the 7th century A.D., three kingdoms vied for supremacy in southern India. The Chalukyas of Badami, the Pandyas of Madurai and the Pallavas of Kanchipuram.[10]

Extent of Pallava Dynasty:

- The Pallava Dynasty had a vast empire with Kanchipuram as the Pallava capital.

- At the height of their power, their territories expanded from the northern part of Andra Pradesh to the river Kaveri in the south.

- The Pallava's authority reduced Cholas to a marginal state during the seventh century.

- Vatapi (Badami) was occupied by the Pallava king Narsimhavarman who defeated Chalukyas. He had got constructed a temple of Lord Vishnu on the steep range of Mahendravari.

- Narsimhavarman was the greatest and the wisest of the Pallavas. He defeated Pulakesin II, the Chalukya ruler. He had established his sovereignty over the entire Deccan. He was the greatest conqueror and a great builder.

- The death of Narsimhavarman brought about an end of the Pallava dynasty towards the end of the 9th century A.D. Aparajita Barman was the last known prince belonging to the imperial line of the Pallavas. He was defeated by the Cholas. With Aparajita, the Pallavas dynasty came to an end.

Rulers of the Pallava Empire:

1. Sibasakanda Varman:

- He was the greatest among the early rulers. He ruled at the beginning of the 4th century A.D.

- He had performed Ashwamedha and other Vedic sacrifices.

2. Simhavarman/Simhavishnu (reign 875 A.D. – 600 A.D.).

- He was a Buddhist i.e. follower of Buddhism religion.

- He included Sri Lanka in his kingdom.

- He defeated the contemporary Tamil ruler. Pallava history assumes a definite character from this ruler onwards.

3. Mahandravarman (reign 600 A.D. – 630 A.D.)

- Succeeded Simhavishnu who was his father.
- He was a poet and imposed vichitrachita and mahavilasa prahasana.
- He introduced rock-cut temple architecture.
- Had on going rivalry and battles with Pulakesin II of Chalukya dynasty.
- Mahendravarman died in battle with the Chalukyas. He was an able and efficient ruler.

4. Narsimhavarman I (630 A.D. – 668 A.D.)

- He was the son and successor of Mahendravarman.
- He is considered as the the greatest of the Pallavas. Also called Narasimhavarman Mahamalla/Mamalla.
- He defeated and killed Pulakeshin II in 642 A.D. He took control of Vatapi, Chalukya capital and assumed the title 'Vitapikvanda'.
- Also vanquished the Cholas, Cheras and the Pandyas.
- He was succeeded by his son Mahandraverman II who ruled from 668 to 670 A.D.

Last rulers:

- After Mahendraverman II, his son Parameshwavarman become the king.
- During his rule, Kanchipuram was occupied by the Chalukyas.
- Nripatunga was an important king who defeated a Pandya king.
- The last ruler of the Pallava dynasty was Aparajitavarman who was killed in a battle against Aditya I, a Chola King in 897 C.E.

Pallava society and culture:

- The Pallava society was based on Aryan culture.

- Brahmins were patronised by the king and they received land and villages. This was called Brahmadeya. The Brahmins' status greatly enhanced during this reign. The caste system became rigid.

- The Pallava king were orthodox Hindus and worshipped Shiva and Vishnu. They were tolerant of Buddhism and Jainism too although both these faiths lost their relevance and popularity.

- Kanchipuram was a great centre of learning. It can be said that the organization of southern India was completed during the Pallava reign.

- There were three types of places during this time:-

    1. **Ur:** where the peasants lived and were headed by a headman who collected and pay the taxes.

    2. **Sabha:** land granted to Brahmins and was also called Agrahara villages. These were tax-free.

    3. **Nagaram:** where merchants and traders resided.

During the Pallavas period, Hindu culture spread to many places in Southeast Asia as well. Pallava influence is evident from the ancient architecture seen in Cambodia and Java.[11]

Pallavas languages:

- All Pallava official works were either in Sanskrit or Prakrit language. Hence can be considered the official languages of the dynasty.

- Some inscriptions were found in Andhra Pradesh and Karnataka in Sanskrit and Prakrit.

- Tamil came to be the language that was mostly used by the Pallavas in their inscriptions, but a few records continued to be in Sanskrit.[12]

Pallavas Religion:

- Pallavas were the followers of Hinduism and made gifts of land to Gods and Brahmins.

- In contact with the frequent customs, some rulers performed the Aswamedha and other Vedic sacrifices.

- The Chinese monk Xuanrang who visited india during the reign of Narasimhavarman I reported that there were 100 Buddhist monasteries and 80 temples in Kanchipuram.[13]

Conclusion: 275 C.E. onwards the Pallavas established themselves as a formidable power in south India. They were able to maintain their rule for approximately 500 years. Pallavas' fortunes declined after Narasimhavarman. The Chalukyan army invaded the Pallava kingdom and threatened Kanchipuram, their capital. Aparajitavaraman was the last king of the Pallava dynasty, and his defeat by the Chola king brought the Pallava power to an end around the end of the 9th century.

CHOLA DYNASTY

Capital: Uraiyur

Official languages: Tamil

Historical era: Ancient Period

Established: 3020 B.C.E.

Rise of the medieval Cholas: 848 C.E.

Empire at its greatest extent: 1030 C.E.

Disestablished: 1279 C.E.

Succeeded by: Pandya dynasty

Cholas (from 860 to 1200 C.E.)

Cholas were the most civilized race of the Deccan. They were a powerful kingdom in the south of India, whose influence extended beyond their territorial domain. The Cholas are remembered as one of the longest-ruling dynasties in the southern regions of India. They became prominent in the 9th century and established an empire comprising the major portion of south India after defeating the Pallavas. They also extended their control in Srilanka and the Malay Peninsula and are thus called 'imperial Cholas'. The inscriptions of the Chola Empire found in the temples have provided detailed information regarding the administration, society, economy and culture of the Chola period. The founder of the imperial Chola line was Vijayala.[14]

Rulers of Cholas:

1. Vijayala (850 C.E.)

- The Cholas greatness was resurrected by the Vijayala Dynasty. Around 850 A.D., Vijayala established the imperial Chola Dynasty, most likely as a vassal of the Pallava king.

- Vijayala occupied Tanjure and made it his capital during the conflict between the Pallava and the Pandyas.

2. Aditya I (871-907) C.E.

- Around A.D. 875 Vijayala was succeeded by his capable son, Aditya I.

- Aditya-I defeated Pallava king Aprajita as well as Konga ruler Parantaka Viranarayana.

- Aditya-I significantly increased the family's power and prestige by deposing Pallava Aparajita Varman and bringing Tondaimandalam under his control around 890 A.D.

- Aditya-I was a devote of Shiva, and he erected several temples in his honour.

3. Parantaka-1 (907 – 955 C.E.)

- Aditya-I was quickly succeeded by his son Parantaka-I, who reigned from 1907 – 955. He annexed the territory of the Pandya king and quickly defeated the Vandambas. He swept away all traces of Pallva's power but was defeated by Rashtrakutas.

- He eventually swept away all traces of Pallava power, extending his authority all the way to Nellore in the North.

4. Parantaka-II/Sundara Chola (957-973 C.E.)

Parantaka II was a Chola emperor. He was also known as Sundara Chola because he was considered the pinnacle of male beauty. He was the son of Arjun Jaya Chola and Kalyani, a princess from the Vaidumba clan, an Andhra dynasty based in the Kurnool and Kadapa districts. When Parantaka-II became king, the Chola kingdom had shrunk to the size of a small principality. The Pandyas in the south had resurrected their fortunes, defeating Chola armies and occupying their ancestral lands.

5. Uttama Chola (973–985 C.E.):

Parantaka Chola-II was succeeded by Uttama Chola. He had several wives. Some of them are Orattanan Sorabbaiyar, Tribhuvana Mahadeviyar etc.

6. Rajaraja-I (Arumolivarman) (985-1014 C.E.):

Rajaraja Chola-I, widely regarded as the greatest king of the Chola empire, reigned between 985-1014 C.E. He had conquered the kingdoms of southern India. He laid the groundwork for the Cholas kingdoms expansion into an empire. He was involved in a number of battles with the Chalukyas in the north and the Pandyas in the south. Rajaraja established the Chalukya Chola dynasty by conquering Vengi. He invaded Srilanka and began the island's century Chola occupation.

7. Rajendra Chola (1014-1044 C.E.)

He succeeded Rajaraja Chola. He was the first to venture to the banks of the Ganges. This period is referred to as the Golden age of the Cholas. After his rule, the kingdom witnessed a widespread downfall.

Administration and Governance:

- During the governance by the Cholas, the entire southern region was brought under the umbrella of a single governing

UNDERSTANDING HISTORY

force. The Cholas ruled in a single governing force. The Cholas ruled in a sustained Monarchy.

- The massive kingdom was divided into provinces which were known as Mandalams.

- Separate governors were given the charge for each Mandalam(Provinces).

- These were further, divided into districts which consisted of tehsils.

- The system of rule was such that each village has a self-governing unit during the era of the Cholas. The Cholas were ardent patrons of art, poetry, literature and dharma, the administration was seen investing in the construction of several temples and complexes with sculpture and paintings.

- The king remained the central authority who would make the major decisions and carry out governance.

Architecture: The Chola kings built many temples throughout their kingdoms. The temples of early Cholas are found in large numbers in the former Pudukottai region. These Chola temples reveal the gradual evolution of Chola art and architecture. The Chola kings earlier built brick temples. Later they built stone temples. Cholas temples like Brihadeshwara temple, Rajarajeshwara temple, and Gangaikonda Cholapuram temple took Dravidian architecture to newer heights. Temple architecture continued to flourish even after Cholas.[15]

<u>VIJAYANAGARA EMPIRE</u>

Capital: Vijayanagara (1336 – 1565)

Common languages: Kannada, Telugu and Sanskrit

Religion: Hinduism

Government: Monarchy

Geographical location today: India

Vijayanagara Empire: The Vijayanagara empire was one of the most powerful kingdoms that rose in medieval times. It was a Hindu empire in the region of south India which consisted of the modern states of Karnataka, Andhra Pradesh, Tamil Nadu, Kerala and some parts of Telangana and Maharastra. The Vijaynagara empire was founded by two brothers i.e. Harihara I and Bukka I. They belonged to Sangama Dynasty. The rise of regional kingdoms in the medieval period started as the Delhi Sultanate weakened. The last dynasties of the Sultanate period i.e. Sayyids and Lodis were very weak rulers who could not maintain the kingdom in the south of the country. By the end of the 13th century, efforts made by the southern powers to fend off the Turkic Islamic invasion resulted in the rise of the empire. At the height, it pushed the sultans of the Deccan beyond the Tungabhadra-Krishna River Doab region, conquered nearly all the south India's leading families, annexed modern- day Odisha (formerly known as Kalinga) from the Gajapati Kingdom, and otherwise established itself as a significant power. The empire saw the rule of four different dynasties: Sangama, Saluva, Tuluva and Aravidu dynasties. The Vijayanagara kingdom signifies a Golden Period for the southern region in every aspect.[16]

The Vijayanagar kingdom was founded in 1336 C.E. by two brothers— Harihara and Bukkaraya— who were the officers under the Kakatiyas and later ministers in the kingdom of the Kampili empire. By the end of the 13th century, the empire had risen to prominence as a result of southern powers attempts to repel Islamic Invasion. This empire lasted till 1646 after a major defeat in the Battle of Talikota in the year 1565 by the combined armies of the Delhi Sultanate.

Sources:

There are many sources which help us to reconstruct the history of Vijayanagara empire. These sources are:

- **Literary sources:**

    1. Rayavachakum by Vishvanatha sathanapati.

2. The forgotten history of Vijayanagara empire by Robert Seawell.

3. The Kannada and Telugu literature, like Manucharitram, Saluvabhyudayam, etc. patronized in the Vijayanagar court, give genealogical, political and social formation.

- **Foreign Accounts:**

   1. Nicholo de Conti visited Vijayanagar during the times of Dev Raya I and gave details about his personality.

   2. Abdul Razzaq from Persia visited during Deva Raya II. He described the beauty of the capital city Hampi.

   3. Domingo Paes and Barbosa visited during Krishna Devaraya's time.

Vijayanagar empire was ruled by four important dynasties and these dynasties are:

   1. Sangama
   2. Saluva
   3. Tuluva
   4. Aravidu

Important Rulers:

Harihara

- In 1336 A.D. Harihara become the ruler of the Sangama dynasty.

- He captured Mysore and Madurai.

- In 1356 A.D. Bukka-1 succeeded him.

Krishna Deva Raya (1509-1529 A.D.)

- Krishna Raya of the Tuluva dynasty was the most famous king of the Vijayanagar empire.

- According to Domingo Paes, a Portugese traveller "Krishna Deva Raya was the most feared and perfect king there could possibly be".

- He conquered Sivasamudram in 1510 A.D. and Raichur in 1512 A.D.

- In 1523 A.D. he captured Orissa and Warrangal.

- His empire extended from the river Krishna in the north to the river Kaveri in the south; Arabian sea in the west to the Bay of Bengal.

His Contributions:

- An able administrator.

- He built large tanks and canals for irrigation.

- He developed naval power by understanding the vital role of overseas trade.

- He maintained friendly relations with the Portuguese and Arab traders.

- He increased the revenue of his government.

- He patronized art and architecture.

The Glories of the Vijayanagar Empire:

Administration:

- Well-organized administrative system.

- The king was the head of all power in the state.

- The council of ministers— To assist the king in the work of administration.

- The empire was divided into six provinces.

- Naik— A Governor was appointed to look after the administrative work in each province.

- The province was divided into districts and districts were further divided into smaller units namely villages.

- Mahanayakacharya: He is an officer and contact point between the villages and the Central administration.

The Army:

The army consisted of the infantry, cavalry and infantry. The commander-in-chief was incharge of the family.

Revenue Administration:

- Land revenue was the main source of income.
- The land was carefully surveyed and taxes were collected based on the fertility of the soil.
- Major importance was given to agriculture and to building dams and canals.

Social life:

- Society was systemized.
- Child marriage, polygamy and Sati were prevalent.
- The king allowed freedom of religion.

Economic conditions:

- Controlled by their irrigational policies.
- Textile, mining, metallurgy perfumery, and other several industries existed.
- They had commercial relations with the islands in the Indian Ocean, Abyssinia, Arabia, Burma, China, Persia, Portugal, South Africa and the Malay archipelago.

The Decline of the Empire:

1. The rulers of the Aravidu dynasty were weak and incompetent. Hence, the decline was sure.

2. Many Provincial Governors become independent and began to rule themselves.

3. The rulers of Bijapur and Golconda seized some areas of Vijayanagar. So, the decline was inevitable.

1.3 ORIGIN AND GROWTH OF MAJOR RELIGIOUS STREAMS: VEDIC, JAINISM, BUDDHISM, BHAKTI AND SUFISM, BRAHMO SAMAJ, ARYA SAMAJ, RELIGIOUS PHILOSOPHY OF SRI AUROBINDO

EARLY AND LATER VEDIC RELIGION

Introduction: The Harappan civilization was followed by another great civilization called Vedic or Rig Vedic civilization (1500-600 B.C.) and culture was known as Vedic culture and completely opposed to it. The Vedic texts are primary sources for the reconstruction of the Vedic culture. The Vedic texts and civilization are believed to be composed by Aryans.

- Vedic civilization is divided into two board parts or divisions:

1. Early Vedic civilization

2. Later Vedic civilization

Vedic Literature: The Vedic literature is the most significant source of information about Vedic civilization. The word "Veda" means knowledge. The Vedic literature has evolved in course of many centuries and handed down from generation to generation by the word of mouth. Later on, they were written down.

- There are four Vedas, which are:

- Rig Veda: It is the oldest Veda and it depicts the life of early Vedic people in India. Its text consists of 1028 hymns which are divided into 10 Mandalas or books. The Upaveda of Rigveda is Ayurveda.

- Sama Veda: The Samaveda or the Veda of Chants. It is an ancient Vedic Sanskrit text that offers musical notations. It contains the famous Dhrupada Raga, later sung by Tansen. Samaveda's Upaveda is Gandharva Veda.

- Yajur Veda: This Veda deals with the procedure for the performance of sacrifices. It is futher divided into Shukla

Yajurveda which contains only mantras and Krishna Yajurveda includes mantras as well as prose explanations. The Upaveda of Yajurveda is Dhanurveda.

- Atharva Veda: It concerns itself with magic spells to ward off evil spirits. It is considered to be unknown Aryan work and its classified into 20 Kandas or books with 711 hymns. Shilpa Veda is the Upaveda of Atharva Veda.

Religion in Early Vedic Period: The religious life of early Vedic people was very simple. The prayers for physical protection and material gains were the main concern of the Rig Vedic people to propitiate Gods. The RigVedic Gods were, generally personifications of different aspects of natural forces such as rain, storm, sun etc. The attributes of these Gods also reflect the tribal and patriarchal of the society. They worshipped a number of Gods and Goddesses in the religion. Indra, Agni, Varuna, Mitra, Dyaus, Pushana, Yama, Soma etc. are all male Gods. Ushas, Sarasvati, Prithvi etc are Goddesses. Among all, Indra was the most popular during the early Vedic period. Indra was also called "Purandar" i.e. breaker of forts. Next in importance after Indra was the Agni who was regarded as an intermediary between Gods and people. Varuna was supposed to be the upholder of natural order. The functions of different Gods reflect their needs in society. Indra was most frequently mentioned in Rig Veda. He was also respected as a weather God who brought rain. Soma was associated with plants and herbs. Soma was also a plant from which intoxicating juice was extracted and drunk while performing sacrifices. Pushan was the God of roads, herdsmen and cattle. Other Gods were similarly associated with other aspects of nature and life.

All these Gods were invoked and propitiated at Yajnas or sacrifices. These sacrifices were organised by chiefs of tribes and performed by priests. It also brought large no. of gifts in the form of Dakshina to the priests.

There was no temple and no idol worship during the early Vedic period. Prayer were offered to the Gods. Ghee, milk and grains were given as offerings. Elaborate rituals were followed during the worship. The features of Indian religion developed much later.

Religion in Later Vedic Period: There were many significant changes in the religion of Later Vedic people. Changes in material life also resulted in a change in their attitude towards Gods and Goddesses too. The early Vedic Gods like Indra, Agni, Surya, Varuna etc now lost their importance. Prajapati (the creator), Vishnu (the protector) and Rudra (the destroyer) which were smaller deities in the early Vedic period become extremely important in the Later Vedic period.

Another important feature was the increase in the frequency and number of the Yagna which generally ended with the sacrifices of a large number of animals. This was probably the result growing importance of a class of the Brahmanas and their efforts to maintain their supremacy in the changing society. The sacrifices that were performed in the early Vedic period were very simple. But the yajnas or sacrifices performed in the later Vedic period were very complicated and expensive. These Yajnas brought to Brahmanas a large amount of wealth in the form of dana and dakshina. Some of the important yajnas were— Ashvamedha, Vajapaya, Rajasuya etc. These yajnas are mentioned in the stories of Mahabharata and Ramayana. These yajnas continued for many days. In the later stage, people began to oppose these sacrifices. A path of good conduct and self-sacrifice was recommended for happiness and welfare in the last section of Vedas called Upnishads. These contains two basic principles of Indian philosophy i.e., Karma and the Transmigration of Soul (i.e., rebirth based on past deeds). According to these texts, real happiness lies in getting Moksha i.e., freedom from this cycle of birth and re-birth. The rise of Buddhism and Jainism was the direct result of these elaborate sacrifices.

UNDERSTANDING HISTORY

Parents: Siddhartharaja (father) and Trishala (mother)

Full name: Vardhamana

Siblings: Nandivardhana

Children: Priyadarshana

Born: 540 B.C.E.; Kshatriyakund, Vaishali, Vajji (present-day Vaishali district, Bihar, India)

Died: 468 B.C.E., India

Jainism is one of the oldest surviving religious traditions of India which was already well-established in the 6th-5th century B.C. Jainism is primarily concerned with purifying and liberating the soul from the perpetual cycle of death and re-birth.

Jainism was founded by Rishabdev. Jainism became a major religion under Vardhaman Mahavira who was the 24th Tirthankara. There were 24 Tirthankaras in Jainism. Rishabdev was the 1st Tirthankara, the 23rd was Parsavnath and the last and major Tirthankara was Mahavira.

- **Life of Mahavira:**

Vardhamana was born around 540 B.C. in Kundagrama; Vaishali. He was born in a Kshatriya Jain family. His father Siddhartha was the chief of the Jnatrika clan. His mother was Trishala a Lichchavi princess and sister of its chief Chetaka. From his childhood, he was attracted to spiritual life. He was given a good education. He was married to Yasodha and had a daughter named Priyadarsana or Annoja. After the death of his parents, he left his home at the age of 30 and wandered about as a mendicant for 12 years. He practised various austerities. After 13 months of his ascetic life, he discarded his garments. During the course of his wanderings, he met Ghosala and spent 6 years with him. Ajavika sect was founded by Ghosala. At the age of 42, Vardhaman attained supreme knowledge and become "Kevalin". He then came to be known as "Jina", "Mahavira" or "Great

Hero". He became a Tirthankara. According to Jaina traditions, he attained supreme knowledge under a sal tree at a place called Jimbhikagrama on the bank of river Rijupalik. On the attainment of knowledge, he become a missionary and began to spread the message of his new religion. He visited many places like Champa, Rajagriha, Vaishali etc. Many kings of his time adopted the new religion. At the age of 72, he died in 468 B.C. at Pava, Patna district of Bihar.[17]

Tenets of Jainism: The central tenet of Jainism is non-violence. No other religion lays as much emphasis on non-violence as does as Jainism. It also criticises human emotions. It rejected the authority of Vedas and other Vedic rituals. It denies the existence of God.

In its early stages, deities was not worshipped in Jainism. It emphasises that salvation cannot be attained by worshipping God or by sacrifices. It is an unorthodox religion. According to Jainism, the world has no beginning or end. It goes through a series of progress and decline according to eternal law. Jainism advocates dualism: the world is made of soul (jiva) and matter (ajiva), which are eternal. The coming together of jiva and ajiva creates karma (action) which leads to an endless cycle of birth and rebirth. To free oneself from karma, one has to practice severe austerities and self-mortification.

Triratnas: According to Jainism, Moksha can be attained by following three principles called Triratnas or three Genres. The Jains are required to follow, these principles. There are:

1. Right faith (Samyak-darshana)

2. Right knowledge (Samyak-jnana)

3. Right conduct (Samyak-Charitra)

Five great vows: The monks have to undertake the five great vows (Pancha-mahavrata)

- Ahimsa (Non-violence): The first major vow taken by Jains

- is to cause no harm to other humans and all living beings. This is the highest ethical duty in Jainism.

 UNDERSTANDING HISTORY

- Satya (Truth or not to lie): This vow is to always speak the truth. Neither lie nor speak what is not true and also do not encourage others to speak an untruth.

- Asetya (Non-stealing): A person should not take anything that is not willingly given. Additionally, a Jain person should ask for permission if something is being given.

- Brahmacharya (Celibacy): It means abstinence from sexual pleasures.

- Aparigraha (Non-possessiveness): This includes non-attachment to material things.

The above 4 principles were given by Parshavnatha; the 23rd Tirthankara and the 5th one was given by the last and 24th Tirthankara or Guru i.e. Lord Mahavira.

Sacred books: The sacred books of Jainism are collectively known as Agam or Agam Sutras. It consists of the teachings of Lord Mahavira. These are the teachings that were methodically compiled by his students. They orally compiled the preaching of Lord Mahavir into twelve main texts.

Spread of Jainism: To spread the teachings of Jainism, Mahavira organized an order of his followers that admitted both men and women. He preached his teachings in Prakrit; the language of common people. The followers of Mahavira were not large in number; they were just 14000. The rapid spread of Jainism was due to the dedicated work of the sangha. Jainism gradually spread into the south and west India; where the Brahmanical section was weak.

Traditions stated that the spread of Jainim in Karnataka is attributed to Chandragupta Maurya. The emperor become a Jaina, gave up his throne and spent the last year of his life in Karnataka as a Jaina ascetic; but any other source does not corroborate this tradition. Another reason that was believed to exist behind the spread of Jainism was the great famine in Magadha after the death of Mahavira. The emigrant Jainas also spread Jainism in complete India, including the southern part.

Splitting of Jainism: The split in Jainism started forming about 3rd century B.C.E. The division occurred mainly due to famine in Magadha which Compelled a group led by Bhadrabahu to move to south India. This group was called Shvetambara means "white-clad" i.e. they wear white clothes. Another group was called Digambara means "sky-clad" i.e. naked and they moved to north India under Sthulbhadra.

Svetambara believes that the practice of nudity is not essential to attain liberation. Therefore they wear white clothes. Digambara, on the contrary, believes that in order to achieve nirvana or liberation, one must renounce everything including clothes. Therefore Digambara monks are completely naked.

After the end of the famine, when the southern group came back to Magadha, the changed practices led to the division of Jainism into two sects:

- Digambara

- Svetambara

- **Digambara:** Monks of this sect believe in complete nudity. Male monks donot wear clothes while female monks wear unstitched plain white sarees.

  These follow all five vows.

  Believe women cannot achieve liberation.

  Bhadrabahu was an exponent of this sect.

Major sub-sects:

Mula Sangh

Bisapantha

Terapantha

Taranpatha or Samaiyapantha

Minor sub-sects:

Gumanapatha

Totapantha

- **Svetambara:** Monks of this sect wear white clothes.

  They follow only 4 vows (except Brahmacharya)

  They believe women can achieve liberation.

  Sthulabhadra was exponent of this sect.

Major sub-sects:

Murtipujaka

Sthanakvasi

Terapanthi

Jain councils: There were two main Jain councils held.

First Jain Council: Held at Patliputra in the 3rd century B.C and was presided over by Sthulbhadra.

Second Jain Council: Held at Vallabhi in 512 A·D and was presided over by Devardhi Kshmasramana. The final compilation of Jain literature called Twelve Angas was completed in this council.

Decline of Jainism: The absence of royal patronage, the split among Jains as Digambaras and Swetambaras, lack of missionary zeal, factionalism, the severity of practices, and the spread of Buddhism as a rival faith led to the decline of Jainism.

RELIGION BUDDHISM

Born: Siddhartha Gautama; 563 B.C.E. ; Lumbini, Shakya Republic

Died: 483 B.C.E. (aged 80); Kushinagar, Malla Republic (According to Buddhist tradition)

Spouse: Yashodhara

Children: Rāhula

Parents: Śuddhodana (father) and Maya Devi (mother)

Known for: Founding Buddhism

Other names: Gautama Buddha, Shakyamuni ("Sage of the Shakyas")

Predecessor: Kassapa Buddha

Successor: Maitreya

Buddhism also known as Buddha Dharma and Dharmavinaya, is an Indian religion based on teachings attributed to the Buddha. It originated in Northern India in the 5th century B.C, and gradually spread throughout much of Asia. Gautam Buddha was the founder of this new religion.

Buddha - Biography: Gautam Buddha was born to Suddhodana (chief of republican sakya clan) as Siddhartha in 563 B.C.E. on Vaishakha Poornima day at Lumbini (Nepal). He lost his mother (Mahamaya) just a few days after his birth and after that he was brought up by his stepmother Gautami. There were 32 birth marks on his body. He was given a proper education and he also excelled in archery and other games. He lived a life of comfort in his early years.

He was married to Yashodhara at the early age of 16 and had a son named Rahula. At the age of 29, he left his palace and decided to become a wanderer. He left his palace with horse Kanthaka and then wandered for six long years in search of truth.

He first meditated with Alara Kalama and then Uddaka Ramaputta but later he was not convinced with their teachings. He, later on, joined five wandering ascetics—Assaji, Mahanama, Vappa, Bhadriya and kondanna.

He saw the Four Great Signs which led him to think of renouncing worldly life i.e., an old man, a cripple, an ascetic and a Corpse (a dead body). Finally, he attained "Nirvana" (knowledge) at Bodhgaya sitting under a Pipal tree on the bank of the river Niranjana. At Urvela, he practised rigorous penance and when he was on the point of death due to starvation he was saved by a milkmaid named Sujata. He attained truth at Bodhgaya after meditation and came to be known as "Buddha" or "Enlightened one". He then proceeded to spread the message of his knowledge to the people. He became a missionary and delivered his first speech or sermon at Sarnath near Banaras. He converted a number of people to his new religion. He spread his ideas far and wide. At the age of 80, he died and attained Parinirvana at Kusinagara. His last words were-"All composite things decay, strive diligently."[18]

The five forms that represent Buddha are:

- Lotus and Bull: Birth

- Horse: Renunciation

- Bodhi Tree: Mahabodhi

- Dhammachakra Pravartana: First sermon

- Footprints: Nirvana

Tenets of Buddhism: Buddha asked his followers to avoid the two extremes of indulgence in worldly pleasure and the practice of strict abstinence and asceticism. He described instead the 'Madhyam Marg' or the middle path which has to be followed. According to him, everyone was responsible for their own happiness in life. The main teachings of Buddhism are encapsulated in the basic concept of four noble truths or Ariya-Sachchani and eight fold path or Astangika Marg.

Four Nobel Truths:

- Suffering (dukkha or sorrow) is the essence of the world.

- Every suffering has a cause- Somudya.

- Suffering could be extinguished - Nirodha.

- It can be achieved by following Astanginka Marga (Eight fold path).

Eight Fold Path: The path consists of various interconnected activities related to knowledge, conduct and meditative practices-

- Right view

- Right intention

- Right speech

- Right Action

- Right livelihood

- Right mindfulness

- Right effort

- Right concentration

Dukkha and its extinction are central to Buddha's doctrine. The essence of Buddhism is the attainment of enlightenment. It points to a way of life that avoids self-indulgence. There is no supreme God or deity in Buddhism. The ultimate goal was the attainment of Nirvana which was not a place but an experience that could be attained. Buddha also established a code of conduct for both monastic order and the laymen to follow which are also known as the Five Precepts and refrain from them.

- Violence

- Stealing

- Sexual Misconduct

- Lying or Gossip

- Taking intoxicating substances.

Major Buddhist texts:

The Buddha's teachings were oral. He taught for 45 years; adapting the teaching to suit the group he was addressing. The teachings were rehearsed and authenticated at the first council and were written in Pali language around 25 B.C.E.

Three Pitakas:

- Vinaya Pitaka

- Sutta Pitaka

- Abhidamma Pitaka.

Other important Buddhist texts include Divyavadana, Dipavamsa, Mahavamsa, Milind Panho etc.

Buddhist Councils:

Buddhist councils marked important turning points in early Buddhism. In total, 4 major Buddhist councils were convened after the death of Gautam Buddha:

Council	Patron	Venue	Chairman	Date
1st	Ajatshatru	Rajgriha	Mahakasyapa	483 B.C.
2nd	Kalashoka	Vaishali	Sabakami	383 B.C.
3rd	Ashoka	Pataliputra	Moggaliputta Tissa	250 B.C.
4th	Kanishka	Kundalvana (Kashmir)	Vasumitra and Asvaghosa (Deputy Chairman)	72 A.D.

Schools of Buddhism: Buddhism was divided into two main sects namely Mahayan & Hinayana.

1. Mahayana: It is one of the two main schools of Buddhism. The term Mahayana is a Sanskrit term which literally means "Greater vehicle". It believes in the heavenliness of Buddha and Idol worship of Buddha and originated in Northern India & Kashmir and then spread into central Asia, East Asia and some areas of southeast Asia.

Buddhist schools embedded in China, Korea, Japan & Tibet belong to the Mahayana tradition.

2. Hinayana: It literally means "Lesser vehicle", also known as "Abandoned Vehicle" or "Defective vehicle". It believes in the original teachings of Buddha. It doesn't believe in idol worship and tries to attain salvation through self-discipline & meditation.

Reasons for the spread of Buddhism:

Buddhism gained wide acceptance and popularity and spread like wildfire throughout India with the support of emperor Ashoka, it spreads its wing to central Asia, west Asia & Srilanka. Various causes for the rise and spread of Buddhism are:

- Liberal/Democratic: Unlike Brahmanism, it was far more liberal and democratic. It welcomed people of all castes and even women were admitted also.

- Simple language: The Buddha spread his message in simple language of the masses. The Pali language which Buddha used was spoken by the masses.

- The personality of Buddha: The personality of Buddha encouraged people to adopt his religion. He was very kind and egoless. His simple philosophy drew the attention of the masses.

- Royal patronage: Royal patronage of Buddhism was also responsible for its rapid rise. Kings like Ashoka, Kanishka, Bimibisara etc. patronised Buddhism and helped to spread this religion outside as well.

- Inexpensive: Buddhism was inexpensive, without the expensive rituals that characterised the Vedic religion. It advocated the spiritual path without any material possession.

Buddhism tried to mitigate the evils resulting from the new material life of the 6th Century B.C. Buddhism asked people not to accumulate wealth, and not indulge in cruelty.

Reasons for Decline: From the early 12th century, Buddhism began to disappear. Buddhism faced divisions from time to time. The divisions into various groups like Hinayana and Mahayana pushed it to lose its originality. The simplicity was lost and it was becoming complex. Pali, the spoken language of most people of India, was the medium for the spread of Buddhism. But Sanskrit was used after the 4th council of Buddhism which was held during the reign of Kanishka (the famous ruler of the Kushana Dynasty). Sanskrit replaced it.

Image worship was started in Buddhism by Mahayana Buddhists. In the course of time, there was a rise in Brahamanical faith again. The Muslim Invasion of India almost wiped out Buddhism. Their invasions become regular and forced the Buddhist monks to seek shelter in Nepal and Tibet. All these factors led to the decline of Buddhism in India; the land of its birth.

BHAKTI AND SUFISM

Bhakti and Sufi movements are the two most prominent movements in Hinduism and Islam respectively. The Bhakti movement is a tradition that has its roots in Hindu religion, while Sufism is an Islamic practice that refers to a wide range of mystical and religious movements.

In the medieval period, religion provided the framework of society at the community and state levels. The state allowed intellectual activity to grow to begin with but later curtailed it for reasons of state policy, though it remained confined to discrete groups and was made a subject for philosophical reasoning and logical disputation. As a result, religions failed to play the role of bringing about a harmonious process of living people therefore, had to develop their own beliefs and practices. Sufi and Bhakti represented people's revolt against the ossified practices, in search of and as an endeavour to bring harmony in life. Sufism played the most important role in working out the great synthesis.

1. Bhakti Movement: The most powerful characteristic of the medieval age in India was the Bhakti movement. The movement began in the sixth-seventh century in south India. With the rise of Hindu devotional cults, it gradually spread throughout the country. It was the direct result of the influence of the spread of Islam in India. The cult also emerged as a strong platform against casteism. It was purely based on devotion to God and nothing else. Devotion means Bhakti through which one can realise God. The chief exponents of this cult were Ramanuja, Nimbaraka, Ramnanda, Vallabhacharya, Kabir, Nanak and Srichaityana. They preached the doctrine of love and devotion to realise God. The concept was not new to Indians. It is very much present in the Vedas, but it was not emphasized during the early period. Much later during the Gupta period, when the worship of Lord Vishnu developed, many holy books including the Ramayana and Mahabharata were composed depicting the love and mystical union of the individual with God. The Ramayana, and the Mahabharata, though written earlier were re-written during the Gupta times. Therefore, Bhakti was accepted along with jnana and karma, as one of the recognised roads to salvation. But this way was not popularised at the end of the 14th century in India.

Development in South India: The development of the Bhakti movement took place in Tamil Nadu between the 7th and 12th C.E. It was reflected in the emotional poems of the Nayanars (Devotee of Shiva) and Alvars (devotees of Vishnu). These saints looked upon religion not as cold formal worship but as a loving bond based upon love between worshipped and worshipper.

Development in North India: These saints wrote in local languages, Tamil and Telugu were therefore, able to reach out to many people. They also translated Sanskrit words in local languages. Sanskrit, which was prevalent in the north, was given a new form as the movement moved to North. Bhagavata Purana was a significant work in the 9th century and an important component of Bhakti movement. Kabir, Namadev and Guru Nanak had preached devotion to a Nirankar form of God. The followers of Guru Nanak called themselves as Sikhs.

Important Leaders of the Bhakti Movement:

Nama Deva and Ramanand (Maharashtra and Allahabad): Both of them taught the concept of four varnas and disregarded the ban on people of different castes cooking together and sharing meals.

Sankara and Ramanuja: The propounders of Advaita (non-duality) and Vishishta Advaita (qualified non-duality) respectively. They believed God to be nigun parabrahma and satguna parabrahma respectively.

Vallabhacharya: The propounder of Shuddha Advaita or pure non-duality.

Chaityana: He relied on the use of music, dance and bhajans to get in touch with God. Love was the watchword of the cult.

Kabir: Sant Kabir Saheb also known as 'Kabir Das' and 'Kabir Saheb' was born in 1398, in Varanasi. He was brought up in a Muslim weaver family by Niru and Nima. He was a mystic poet, a musician and one of the important saints of Hinduism. He was also considered a Sufi by Muslims. He is respected by Hindus, Muslims and Sikhs.

He was a disciple of Saint Swami Ramananda. He was never formally educated and was almost completely illiterate. He was a disciple of Ramananda, raised by a Muslim weaver. He stood for doing all way with all unnecessary customs and rituals in both religions and bringing union between these religions. He wrote Sabad, Bijak, Doha, Rekhtal. He propagated Ram Bhakti.

Nimbakacharya: He was the founder of the Radha-Krishna cult. He expressed the relation to substantiate the importance of marriage. It was also used as an example of God's love for people.

Result of the Bhakti Movement: The results of the Bhakti Movement were far reaching. The first and foremost result was that it minimized the differences between Hindus and Muslims. The people of one religion tried to understand the feelings of the people of another religion.

Secondly, the caste system gradually lost its importance as the Bhakti preachers disregarded it.

Thirdly, the spiritual life of the people became very simple and more developed than before.

Lastly, the movement had a tremendous impact on the literature and language of the country. It helped the regional languages to get enriched and this movement has an everlasting influence on the people of India and outside.

The Vaishnavite Movement: Apart from the non-sectarian movement led by the Kabir and Nanak, the Bhakti movement in North India developed around the worship of Rama and Krishna, the two incarnations of God Vishnu. Tulsidas was the worshipper of lord Rama and the embodiment of the supreme reality. In 1585 C.E., the followers of the Krishna cult founded the Radha Ballabhi sect under Harivamsa. A popular bhakti saint, Vallabhacharya popularised the Krishna bhakti cult in the Telangana region. Surdas was the disciple of Vallabhacharya and he popularised the Krishna cult in North India. He wrote "Sursagar" in Brajbhasha which is full of verses on the charm of Lord Krishna and his beloved Radha. Mirabai was a great devotee of Krishna and she became popular in Rajasthan for her bhajans.

Chaitanya was another well-known saint and social reformer of Bengal who popularised the Krishna cult. He is said to have travelled all over India, including Vrindavan where he revived this cult. He popularized the Kirtan system, group devotional songs accompanied by ecstatic dancing. He believed that through love and devotion, song and dance, a devotee can feel the presence of God. He did not reject the scriptures or idol worship though he cannot be defined as as classified traditionalist.

2. Sufi Movement: Sufism was a liberal reform movement within Islam. It had its origin in Persia and spread into India in the 11th century. The first Sufi saint Sheikh Ismail of Lahore started preaching his ideas. It can be traced to Abu Hamid-al Ghazali who belonged to the Ashari school which reconciled with mysticism and led a Sufi life. His influence led to the setup of Madrasas (schools) and Velma (scholars). Sufism stressed the elements of love and devotion as effective means of the realisation of God. Love of God means love of humanity and so Sufis believed service to humanity was tantamount to service to God. In Sufism, self-discipline was considered an essential component to gain knowledge of God by the sense of perception. While other orthodox Muslims emphasised external conduct, the Sufis lay stress on inner purity. Orthodox believe in blind observance of rituals, the Sufis considered love and devotion as the only means of attaining salvation. According to them, one must have the guidance of a pir or guru, without which spiritual development is impossible. Sufism also inculcated a spirit of tolerance among its followers. Other ideas emphasised by Sufism are meditation, good actions, the performance of prayers, fasting, charity and suppression of passion by ascetic practices.

  UNDERSTANDING HISTORY

They were called Sufis as they wore garments of wool as their budge of poverty. Thus the name is derived from the word 'Suf'. The Sufis did not attach importance to Namaz,Hajj and Celibacy. That is the reason they were misunderstood by orthodox Muslims. There were some leading Sufi saints like Khwaja Moinuddin Chisti, Farid-ud-din Ganj-i-Shakar, Nizam-ud-din Auliya etc..

In India, Sufism adopted many native Indian concepts such as Yogic postures, music and dances. Sufism found adherents among both Hindus and Muslims. The Sufis come to India via Afghanistan. In the beginning, the main centres were Punjab and Multan which later on spread to Kashmir, Bihar, Bengal and Deccan.

There were two broad Sufi orders:

Bashara: those who obeyed Islamic laws.

Beshara: those who were more liberal.

The Beshara were also called 'Mast Kalandar'. They comprised of wandering monks who were also called Baba. They did not leave any written accounts.

By the 12th century, the Sufis were organised in 12 orders or Silsilas. A Silsila was generally led by a prominent mystic who lived in a Khanaqah along with his disciples. The link between the teacher and his disciples was a vital part of the Sufi system. Every pir nominated a successor to carry on his works. In fact, Qawwali developed during this period. The four most popular silsilas were the Chishtis, Suhrawardis, Qadririyas and Naqshbandis.

Chishti Silsila: Established by Khwaja Moin-ud-din Chishti (also known as Gharib Nawaz) around 1192 C.E. After staying in Lahore and Delhi, they shifted to Ajmer which was an important political centre and already had a sizeable Muslim population. His fame grew more after his death. Famous Chishti saints were Farid-ud-din-Ganj-i-Shakar, Nizamuddin Auliya, Muhammad BandaNawaz etc. The Chishtis led a very simple life and conversed with people in their local dialect. They made themselves popular by adapting musical recitations called Sama. Amir Khusrau was a disciple of Auliya.

Suhrawardi Silsila: Founded by Sheikh Shihabuddin Suhrawardi in Baghdad and in India by Bahuddin Zakariyas. Unlike Chishtis, they accepted maintenance grants from Sultans. They believed that Sufis should possess three attributes of property, knowledge and hal (mystical enlightenment). The famous saints were Hamid-ud-din Nagori, Rukh-up-din Abdul Fath.

Qadiri Silsila: Shiekh Nizamatullah, Mukhdum Muhammad Jilani and Miyan Mir and their father Sheikh Abdul Qadir established the Qadiri Silsila during Mughal rule. Popular in Punjab. Qadiris believed in the concept of Wahdat-al-Wajood meaning "Unity of Existence" i.e. God and his creations are one and similar.

Naqshbandi Silsila: Established by Khwaja Bahauddin Naqshbandi. It was popular in North India. The Sufis of this Silsila believed that relationship between man and God was that of slave and master. This sect is orthodox. Famous saints were Shiekh Ahmed Sirhindi, Bubur and Ubaidullah Ahrar.

The Sufis believe in the concept of Wahadat-ul-Wajud (unity of Being). The Hatha Yoga treatise Amrita Kunda was translated into Arabic and Persian. The Sufi saints maintained close contact with the common people. The Sufi saints who were poets chose to write in the local language. The liberal views of Sufis influenced the Din-i-Iilahi of Akbar.

Impact of Sufism: The liberal and unorthodox elements of Sufism had a profound impact on medieval Bhakti saints. In the later period, the Sufi doctrines influenced the religious perspective of the rulers along with reminding them of their moral obligations.

Sufism influenced both rural and urban regions and had a deep political, cultural and social influence on the masses. Spiritual bliss became the ultimate aim and people could raise their voice against all forms of orthodoxy, falsehood etc. In a world torn by strife and conflict, Sufis tried to bring peace and harmony.

The most important contribution of Sufism is that it helped a lot to develop a bond of solidarity and brotherhood between Hindus and Muslim communities. The Sufi saints were not reversed only by Muslims but also by a huge number of Hindus.[19]

Conclusion: Thus we see that Bhakti and Sufi movements created a new spirit in religious life and took on social reforms in creating an egalitarian society. They worked for the poor and downtrodden and believed in personal devotion as a tool to God.

BRAHMO SAMAJ

Foundation of Brahmo Samaj:

Founder: Raja Ram Mohan Roy

Founded: 20 August 1828, Kolkata

Headquarters location: Kolkata

Scripture: Brahmo Dharma

Brahmo Samaj is one of the most powerful socio-religious movements in India. It was launched in Bengal in 1828. It is an assembly of all sorts and descriptions of people without distinction, meeting publicly for the sober, orderly, religious and devout adoption of "the (nameless) unsearchable eternal, immuntable being who is the author and preserver of the universe". It made a significant contribution to the making of modern India. Raja Mohan Roy is considered as the founder of Brahmo Samaj. The Brahmo Samaj played an important role in stamping out the dowry and caste systems, aiming to encourage women's empowerment. With its success in achieving its objectives, it became a pioneer contributor to Bengal Renaissance.

Raja Ram Mohan Roy: Raja Ram Mohan Roy founded the Brahmo Sabha (later named Brahmo Samaj) on 20 August 1828. He was an Indian reformer and was known as the "father of modern India" and also the "father of Bengal Renaissance."[20]

Raja Ram Mohan Roy was born on the 22nd of May in 1772 in the then Bengal presidency in Radha Nagar in the Hooghly district. His parents were Ramakant Roy and Tarini devi. His brother was Jag Mohan. His early education included the study of Persian and Arabic and he read the Quran. He studied the philosophy of Buddhism, Islam and Hinduism. In Banaras, he studied Sanskrit and read Vedas and Upanishads.

From 1803 to 1814, he worked for the East India Company as a clerk. In 1814, he resigned and moved to Kolkata to devote his life to religious, social and political reforms. He established Atmiya Sabha in 1815. In 1817, he in collaboration with David Hare established Hindu College in Kolkata, India. He also established Vedanta College in 1825. He also started Anglo- Hindu school that insisted on the teaching of monotheistic doctrines. In 1828, he established Brahmo Samaj to spread his ideology like reading Vedas and Upanishads, Christianity is not bad, opposing idol worship, and child marriage, and he made various efforts to end orthodox traditions. In 1829, he abolished Sati with the help of Lord William Bentick (1824-1829), the first Governor General of India. He got the title of "Raja" from Akbar II (the Mughal emperor) and was sent as his envoy to England to meet George IV. He died in 1833 in Bristol, England. The concept of Brahmo Samaj was not restricted to Raja Ram Mohan Roy. It was later joined by other famous reformers. These are as follows:

Brahmo Samaj and Debendranath Tagore:

Debendranath Tagore was leader of Tattavabodhini Sabha. This Sabha was established in 1839. He joined Brahmo Samaj in 1843 and gave a defined structure to the Brahmo Samaj by the informal union of the two with his contribution to the Brahmo Samaj, the introduction of new strength caused its growth. Later many independent thinkers supported it like Ashwini Kumar Datta, Ishwar Chandra Vidyasagar and other followers of Ram Mohan followers. He wanted to bring some reforms into society and thus fought against Christian Missionaries. He emphasized monogamy and was totally against polygamy. He opposed child marriage, idol worship and favoured women's education.

Brahmo Samaj and Keshab Chandra Sen:

The "superstitious practices" Ram Mohan Roy objected included sati, caste rigidity, polygamy and child marriages. Raja Ram Mohan Roy demanded property inheritance rights for women and which was a movement of reformist Bengali's formed to fight against social evils.[21] The Brahmo Samaj led a crusade against the practice of Sati, polygamy, child marriage of minor girls, caste system, purdah system, untouchability and use of intoxicants. It adopted inter-caste marriages, education of women, widow remarriages etc., as practical measures for removing the social evils. It succeeded in creating a general awakening against these social evils in Bengal.[22]

Along with Debendranath Tagore, Keshab Chandra Sen joined Brahmo Samaj in 1858. With his introduction, there was burst of vitality and Brahmo Samaj spread out of Bengal in Punjab, Madras, United Provinces, Bombay and other cities (this was known as the Adi Brahmo Samaj). Because of this, people of the society opposed child marriage of 13-year-old girls with a minor Hindu Maharaja, which resulted in their separation in the Sadharan Brahmo Samaj (founded by Umesh Chandra Dutta, Sib Chandra Deb and Ananda Mohan Bose).

Objectives of Brahmo Samaj: The major objectives of Brahmo Samaj are as follows:

1. Opposition to idolatry.

2. Abolishing practice of Sati (abolished in 1829).

3. Stopping child marriage and polygamy.

4. Raising voice against the degraded status of widows.

5. Propagation of western and modern thoughts in society.

6. It aims at purifying the concept of Hinduism and preaching monotheism.

7. Focusing on meditations, prayers and reading of the scriptures.

Doctrines of Brahmo Samaj: Following doctrines as noted in renaissance of Hinduism, are common to all varities of the Brahmo Samaj:

1. Brahmo Samajists have no faith in any scriptures as an authority.

2. They have no faith in avataras.

3. They denounce polytheism and idol-worship.

4. They are against caste restrictions.

5. Brahmo Samajists make faith in the doctrines of Karma and Rebirth optional.

Divisions of Brahmo Samaj: The Brahmo Samaj was divided into two. These were:

1. Adi Brahmo Samaj: This category of Brahmo Samaj was developed from "Brahmoism" and became the first movement organised in British India. This worked against the wrong ideas of the caste system that differentiated the people based on their caste. It started educating secular India to eradicate the old norms of society. Adi Brahmo Samaj was started by Raja Ram Mohan Roy, Prasanna Coomar Tagore and Debendranath Tagore.

2. Sadharan Brahmo Samaj: The Brahmo Samaj has Schism in its context, which led to the formation of Sadharan Brahmo Samaj. The existence of Sadharan Brahmo Samaj came into being in a public meeting at the Town Hall, Calcutta. The head of this samaj was Anand Mohan. This religious movement was headed by Ananda Mohan Bose, Sib Nath Shastri and Umesh Chandra Dutta.

ARYA SAMAJ

Foundation of Arya Samaj:

Founder: Dayananda Saraswati

Founded: 10 April 1875, Goregaon, Mumbai

Headquarters: New Delhi

President: Suresh Chand Aggarwal

Secretary: Prakash Arya

Arya Samaj was the first reform movement that practised proselytization. Arya Samaj's follower's believed in God's extreme superiority and condemned idol worship. It was founded by Swami Dayanand Saraswati on 10th April 1875 in Bombay. According to the Arya Samaj, Vedas are the ultimate source of knowledge. They educated Hindus about Vedas and helped in fighting for women's empowerment, worked for widow remarriage, child marriage and polygamy. It propagates the universal doctrines of humanity. It is neither a religion nor a sect. The Arya Samaj had its largest following in western and Northern India. The Samaj opposes worship of Murtis, animal sacrifices, shradda, untouchability, child marriage, priestly craft and temple offerings. It upholds the doctrine of Karma and Samsara and programs of social reform. The first meeting of Arya Samaj was held in Bombay in 1875. It not only gave an opportunity to organize Hinduism again but also gave a momentum to the nationalist movement.

Swami Dayanand Saraswati:

Swami Dayanand Saraswati founded the Arya Samaj on April 10 in 1875. He established the Arya Samaj based on two basic tenets and these were:

- Monotheism

- Infalliable authority of the Vedas

Original name of Dayanand Saraswati was Mulshankar. He was born on 12 Feb., 1824 in a Brahmin family in the state of Gujarat. The death of his younger sister and uncle due to cholera led him to ponder the meaning of life and death. Therefore, he left his home at the age of 21 and wandered as an ascetic in search of higher truth. After some time, he met with a religious teacher Virajanand Dandeesha in Mathura and became his disciple. From him, he learned and practised various forms of Yoga. His guru Vrijanand believed that Hinduism had strayed away from its roots and many of its betterment and also to work hard to restore the Hindu faith in Vedas. He emphasized the concept of one God. He was the founder of Vedic schools to educate all the castes; males and females. They give free shelter, clothes etc. He pushed society against the untouchability and inequalities of caste. He worked for the better status of women and the protection of widows. He was a religious and social reformer. He focused on humanity. He was a famous novelist. His notable works included 'Satyartha Paraksh' in the year 1867. In this book, he opposed idol worship, polygamy, Puranas, and child marriage, and favoured inter-caste marriage, equal status for women and widow remarriage. Other books are Rig Veda Bhashyam and many more. Along with Sanskrit, his books were published in foreign languages like English, French, Arabic, German etc.

Swami Dayanand Saraswati founded the Arya Samaj, but the contribution of Pandit Lekh Ram, Shri Shraddhanand etc made the Arya Samaj reach people and spread the real meaning of Hinduism among the masses. Swami Dayanand Saraswati gave the Slogan "Go back to Vedas"

Features of Arya Samaj: Arya Samaj was a socio-religious reform movement founded by Dayanand Saraswati to bring back the ideas of Vedas in the Hindu religion. The key features are as follows:

- Arya Samaj believes God is the supreme power and primary source of all knowledge.

- It states that God is one and it doesn't hold physical existence.

- It was strongly against the cruel practices of animal sacrifices, feeding the dead through Sraddhas etc.

- It supported the concept of soul transmigration and Karma.

- Arya Samaj believes that Veda is not liable to mislead and thus regarded as the knowledge's ultimate source.

- The Samaj was against post-Vedic texts.

- It strongly condemns the domination of Brahmin.

Principles of Arya Samaj:

- Almighty God creates the universe. He is immortal thus it alone needed to be worshipped.

- The genuine scriptures of wisdom are the Vedas.

- A true Arya must be ready to reject the lies and embrace the truth.

- Every individual needs to be treated with respect, justice and compassion.

- Dharma must be the guiding concept for the activities.

- A person must accept knowledge and avoid ignorance.

- Arya Samaj aims to promote every individual's social and physical well-being.

- Every person must take care of their welfare. But, he must consider the welfare of others.

- God create all knowledge.

- Rather than thinking about an individual's well-being, one must think about the collective well-being of humanity.

Controversies in Arya Samaj: To fulfil the aim of opening doors for Vedic knowledge. Arya Samajists took many steps, but all steps did not prove successful. Some of these, created conflicts. One of the biggest controversies associated with Arya Samaj was the Shuddi movement. "Shuddhi" means to re-convert all those who had embraced either Islam or any other religion. They were given an opportunity to come back to their old religion. Arya Samajists adopted the Shuddi programme to bring back the purity of Hindu people influenced by other religions. The movement was against the Christian missionaries. Arya Samaj also worked to protect cows. It also resulted in riots between Hindus and Muslims.

Significance: Arya Samaj brought many changes to the Hindu religion. It works to prevent child marriage and improve the status of women in the country. It has set a minimum age for marriage i.e. 16 years for girls and 25 years for boys. It worked for human welfare. They founded D.A.V (Dayanand Anglo Vedic) colleges. The first college was established in Lahore in 1886. It successfully brought back the self-esteem of Hindus. It helped in eliminating the influence of westernization over Hinduism.

Arya Samaj Around The World: Although Arya Samaj was initially established in Bombay, India. Later on it spreads to other parts of the country with its headquarters in New Delhi. The movement has its roots in India and spread throughout the world in countries involving Kenya, Nepal, Russia, United States, Tanzania, South Africa, Mauritius and a lot more.

RELIGIOUS PHILOSOPHY OF SRI AUROBINDO

Born: 15 August 1872, Kolkata

Died: 5 December 1950, Puducherry

Spouse: Mrinalini Devi

Parents: Swarnalata Devi, Krishna Dhan Ghosh

Full name: Aurobindo Ghosh

Every year on the 15th of August, which coincides with India's Independence Day, Hindus celebrate the birth anniversary of Rishi Aurobindo— the great Indian scholar, reformer, an experimentalist and also a great spiritualist.

Aurobindo Ghosh, popularly known as Shri Aurobindo was born on August 15, 1872, in Calcutta, Bengal presidency of British India, now Kolkata, in West Bengal. His father's name was Krishna Dhan Ghosh a famous member of Brahmo Samaj and his mother's name was Swarnalata Devi. In Sanskrit, the word 'Aurobindo' means Lotus. Aurobindo's father had chosen this name thinking that it was unique; the lotus is the symbol of divine consciousness.

Aurobindo received his early education in a convent school intended for European children and in 1879 was taken by his father to England for schooling in Manchester and later at St. Paul's school, in London. A scholarship from St. Paul enabled Aurobindo to go to King's College, Cambridge, in 1889. He practically won all the prizes in Greek and Latin. He passed the first part of classical Tripos in the

                                UNDERSTANDING HISTORY

first class in 1892. The same year he passed his Indian Civil Services examination successfully but he did not report for the riding and thereby was disqualified for the civil services.

Shri Aurobindo, who had started writing at an early age, even during his study at Manchester, had continued with his creativity through all the turbulent phases of his life. After returning back to India in 1893, he joined Baroda College as a professor of English in the princely state of Baroda. He knew many languages such as Bengali, English, Latin, German, French, Greek, Italian, Spanish, Gujarati, Marathi, Sanskrit and Hindi. Later on, in 1905 he gave up Baroda College and joined as principal of Bengal National College. He also joined Indian National Congress for Independence and become an active freedom fighter. He started the journal 'Bandematram' to publish revolutionary views. He was influenced by the study of Vedas, Upanishads, Ramayana, Mahabharata, Gita and spiritual literature and engaged most of his time in practising Yoga and meditation during jail time. He passed away on December 5, 1950 in Pondicherry.

Shri Aurobindo's philosophy on life is mainly based on "Vedas", "Upanishads", "Mahabharata" of Ved Vyas and Patanjali's "Yogasutra" and last but not the least the teachings of "Bhagavad Gita". He was initially an idealistic person. His philosophy of education is based on idealism, realism, naturalism, spiritualism, humanism, nationalism and internationalism.

Very few researchers have been developed to study spiritual education with respect to Shri Aurobindo's philosophy in India and its contribution to field of education in less explored. Shri Aurobindo feels that "The true basis of education is the study of mind". For the appearance of spirituality in the development of education, Kothari Commission (1966) in this connection points out, "In the men, material affluence and power would be subordinated to that of higher values and fulfilment of the individual." This concept of the mingling of 'science and spirituality' is of special significance for Indian education.

Moral and Religious Education by Aurobindo Gosh: Shri Aurobindo puts emphasis on moral and religious education besides intellectual training, the development of moral and religious nature is an essential point of the education of the "complete man". In the words of Shri Aurobindo, "in the economy of man, the mental nature rests upon the moral and the education of the intellect divorced from the protection of the moral and emotional nature checks human progress. A lack of moral and religious education tends to corrupt the human race. Morality and religion are all theoretical. It will not make a man moral and religious in reality. It may not vanity and delusion because the heart is not necessarily educated by instructing the mind.

According to Shri Aurobindo, morality consists of acting in accordance with the moral law. Moral life consists of controlling impulses and instincts and forming wholesome habits.

As Shri Aurobindo believes, the four components of moral nature are:-

- Emotions
- Formed habits
- Formed Associations
- Innate Nature

Hence the pupil should be guided to cultivate–

- Right emotions
- Noble habits
- Right association
- Right action to be followed by his nature.

Techniques for imparting moral education are as follows:

Direction and Encouragement: The best way to help the child is to put him on the right road to his own perfection and to encourage him to follow it. In no way, the child should be interfered within this process. Children should be encouraged to analyse their bad qualities and cultivate good qualities.

Suggestion: In moral training, it is the suggestion that could be more helpful and not commands and impositions. The personal example in all walk of life within the reach of the child is the best suggestion. "An example that is better than percept" is a well known proverb. The teacher should be a man of integrity and noble ideas.

Opportunities for action: The child should be given an opportunity to put into action the moral impulses that arises within him. Qualities which form a moral attitude of our young man are "The thirst for knowledge, the self-devotion, the purity. The renunciation of the Brahmin, the courage, ardour, honour, nobility, chivalry, the patriotism of Kshatriya, the beneficence, skill, industry, general enterprise and large open handedness of Vaishya, the self-effacement and loving service of the in Shudra". For developing this attitude it is essential to train our young men in the Aryan traditions.

Yoga: Moral training can be supplemented by the application of the kind of yoga called Raja Yoga which aims at the purification of the mind and body. With regard to religion, Shri Aurobindo says that religion literates man from slavery. It emancipates man from falsehood and gives us the divine health of courage and nobility. The teaching of dogmas to children is no religious training worth the name because dogmas cannot help them to be pious and moral. Shri Aurobindo says, "The essence of religion is to live for God, for humanity, for the country, for others and for oneself". It is the religious ideal that must be made an essential part of every school and college. In fact, religion must be lived and experienced. No religious coaching is valuable unless it is lived and experienced. Religion is to be lived, not learned as a creed to use for various kinds.

1.4 DEVELOPMENT OF LITERARY TRADITIONS: PANINI, KALIDAS, VEDVYAS, VALMIKI

Traditional literature is a genre that started in the oral traditions. Myths, fables, epics, ballads, legends, folk rhymes, folktales, tall tales, etc. are part of this genre. The earliest Indian literature took the form of Hindu sacred writings which were known as Vedas written in Sanskrit. Ramayana and Mahabharata are also from ancient Indian literature. A large number of literary works were written later on. Ancient literature comprises scientific and religious documents; tales, poetry and other forms of writings that were recorded on a variety of things like stones, palm leaves and metals.

PANINI

Parents: Dakshi, Panin

Full name: Daksiputra Pānini

Siblings: Pingala

Era: 4th century B.C.E.; 400–350 B.C.E.; 6th–5th century B.C.E.

Main interests: Grammar, linguistics

There are hardly any written records or biography of Panini as such that have information on the time he was born. It is however estimated that he was born around 4th,5th or 6th century B.C. There are different opinions of historians regarding these dates. It is also said that he was born in Shalatula, near Indus river. This place at present is in Pakistan. Experts and historians, however, base these dates on pure guesswork. Also, there is hardly any proof or evidence regarding the extend of his work. Sanskrit is considered to be a classical language of India most of the language spoken in the Indian sub-continent are derived from Sanskrit. In Sanskrit language, grammar is considered to be a very important part. It was thought of as a distinctive field of scientific study. It was considered a kind of field that had its own parameters and set of rules and Panini is considered to be the creator of this language. He was a Sanskrit grammarian who gave comprehensive and scientific theory of phonetics phonology and morphology.

After Panini's work, Patanjali's "Mahabhashya" is considered one of the most important work in the field of Sanskrit grammar. Patanjali gave Indian linguistic science a much-needed development at the time. He developed the system of Shiksha and Vyakarana. Panini's grammar is considered to be the world's first formed system of language. It was vented way before Gottlab Frege's innovations in language in 19th century. India honoured him by releasing a stamp of him in the year 2004. A temple named as Panini Smarak Mandir is present in the region of Kasha, built with soil brought from Pakistan, where he was born. Not much information is available about Panini's personal life. It is said that his mother was called "Daksi" and his uncle from his mother's side was called "Vyadi". Not much is known about his father but according to historians his name was Pani but some are against it. His brother is known to be Pingali.

Major Works: Panini was one of the most inventive and original people who helped in the development of knowledge of Sanskrit grammar. He is considered to be the founder of literature and language. This famous Sanskrit grammarian gave a scientific analysis of Sanskrit phonetics and morphology. Being the language of Gods, Sanskrit was considered to be a complete and perfect language. He analyzed the classical Sanskrit language, which was the language of all literary works and more light was thrown on the phonology of the language. Among Panini's works, the most famous and major one is called "Ashtadhyayi". It is a thesis and consists of 8 chapters and each of them is divided into quarter chapters. This treatise basically highlights the difference between the language of holy texts and the language used for communicating in normal lives. A basic set of rules and grammar was given to describe Sanskrit grammar. He went on step by step and explained the use of nouns, verbs and vowels and divided them into classes and then went on to explain the construction of sentences and the use of compounds, nouns and tenses. It is very similar to the principles of mathematics as the construction of these grammatical patterns functions mathematically.

Impact on Europe And Other Parts: Panini's work had quite an impact on modern linguistics. In the 19th century, Europe got to know about Panini's work. It was mainly Franz Bopp who started taking interest in his work. Later on, many more modern times linguistics get influenced by his work. He is known as the "Father of modern structural linguistics". He has himself confessed on many occasions that Indian grammar and structure had a lot of influence on his work and thinking.

KALIDASA

Notable works: Kumārasambhavam, Abhijñānaśākuntalam and Raghuvamśa

Period: 4th–5th century C.E.

Language: Sanskrit, Prakrit

Subject: Epic poetry, Puranas

One of the greatest Sanskrit poets that India has ever had, the life history of Kalidas is absolutely fascinating and interesting. Though the exact time of his fame is not known, it is estimated that he survived around the middle of the 4th or 5th century A.D. He was a Sanskrit poet. He is well known as the greatest poet of all time. His works are mainly on "Vedas", "Ramyana" and "Mahabharat". The biography of the great Indian poet provides us with an immense amount of information about the places he travelled and the kind of life he led.

Kalidas might live in the Himalayas. The work "Kumar Sambhava" by poet Kalidas displays his interest in Himalayas and the city of Ujjain which shows he might have lived in the place. Some other poets wrote in their works about his birthplace. His birth and death are not exactly traceable, according to some books we came to know that he lived in Kashmir and then moved towards the south. His birth and death are notably not recorded in any of the books, but some hypothetical years of estimation are made. His birth took place in the 4th century C.E. and he died between the 4-5th century.

The poems he wrote were usually of epic proportions and were written in classical Sanskrit. His creations were used for fine arts like music and dance. He is regarded as an outstanding writer, Kalidasa resides at the palace of Chandragupta in Pataliputra (Now Patna). He was one of the gems of the court of Chandragupta. According to legends, Kalidasa was blessed with good looks. This attracted a princess with whom he fell in love. Since Kalidas was not good in intellect and wit, the princess rejected him. He then worshipped Goddess Kali and she blessed him with intellect and wit and thus making him one of the "nine gems" in the court of Chandragupta. He is also known as "Indian Shakespeare".

Major works: Shakuntlam: The most famous and beautiful work of Kalidas is the "Shankuntlam". It is the second play of Kalidas after he wrote "Malavikagnimitra". The Shankuntlam tells the story of king Dushyant who fell in love with a beautiful girl "Shankuntala", the daughter of a saint. They get married and both lived happily with each other until one day, the king is asked to travel somewhere. In his absence, a sage curses Shakuntala as she offends him unknowingly by not acknowledging his presence. Due to the curse, Dushyanta's entire memory is wiped off and he doesn't remember his marriage with Shankuntala. But the sage feels pity for her and gives a solution that he will remember everything if he sees the ring that he has given to her. She lost her ring in the river while bathing. After a series of incidents, a fisherman who finds the ring inside a fish rushes to the king with the ring. The king then recalls everything and rushes to Shankuntala to apologize for his actions. She forgives him and they live happily ever after.

He also wrote 'Raghuvasma' which describes the entire family tree of Raghuvasma starting from Dilipa to Rama.

He wrote a poem called "Meghaduta".

A major epic written by poet Kalidas is "Kumarasambhava" which contains many poems and the birth history of Goddess Parvati. "Meghaduta" is one of the finest works of Kalidas in terms of world literature. The beauty of the continuity in flawless Sanskrit is unmatched to date.

Minor works: Kalidasa wrote some Khandakavyas along with major works. Khandakavyas are smaller poems. He wrote a Khandakavyas on Ritusambara which describes the six seasons. The most popular plays of ancient times are the plays written by Kalidasa.

Kalidas works revolve around the following things:

- Expressing the love of nature.
- Praising the seasons and monsoons.
- Glorifying the field and sky.
- Illustrating the mother earth.

His works demonstrate majorly nature. His works include soul-satisfying peace. His works are almost similar to the work of Shakespeare. Hence is called "Indian Shakespeare". Many works of Kalidas poetry are translated into local languages. With his simplistic and lucid style of writing, he brought Sanskrit poetry to a level that has rarely been surpassed in Indian history. The oldest paleographical evidence of Kalidas in 473 C.E. is the inscription from the Sun Temple. Later Kalidas Sanskrit plays inspired European literature in the late 18th and early 19th centuries.

He is widely regarded as greatest Sanskrit poet and dramatist of all time. In recognition of what Kalidas wrote, the Indian government gives Kalidas Samman in Madhya Pradesh who performs well in classical dance, poetry, classical music, plastic arts and other art forms.

VEDA VYASA

Born: Kalpi

Full name: Krishna Dvaipayana Veda Vyasa

Parents: Satyavati, Parāśara

Children: Vidura, Shuka, Dhritarashtra, Pandu

Known for: Mahabharata

The life history of Veda Vyas is an interesting one. The author of the great epic "Mahabharata", Veda Vyas was the first and greatest Acharya of Sanatana Dharma. He is responsible for classifying the four Vedas, he wrote the 18 Puranas and recited the great Mahabharata. In fact, the Mahabharata is often called the fifth Veda. The most important and most glorified section is the Bhagavad Gita, the lesson recited to Arjuna by Lord Krishna on the battlefield. Apart from Mahabharata, he also wrote the Brahma Sutra, one of his shortest theologies on Hindu philosophy. Seeing the widespread violence in today's time; he is said to have retreated into some remote village in northern India. The life of Veda Vyas is an example to all in modern times of how to be selfless and devote oneself entirely to the lord in order to attain Nirvana.

He is also known as Krishna Dvaipayna. Around some 5000 years ago he was born in Damauli of Tanahi District, which is now in Nepal. He wrote Mahabharata which still exists in Nepal. Parashar Rishi was his father and Satyavati was his mother. He taught the Vedas to his pupils with ardent devotion and dedication. It is said that Mahabharata is the 18th Purana that was written by Veda Vyas. He fathered four famous sons Pandu, Dhritarashtra, Vidur and Sukhdev. Veda Vyas received knowledge from great sages like Vasudev and Sanakadik. He described that the most important goal in one's life is to attain Narayana or the Divine supreme.

Major works:

Mahabharata: It is the worlds largest epic and longest epic of India written by Veda Vyas. He is considered a part incarnation of Lord Vishnu. It is said that he came to the earth in Dwaparyuga to put all the Vedic knowledge in this universe in the form of written words and make it available to everyone. Vedic knowledge existed only in the form of spoken words before Veda Vyas. Veda Vyas was the grandfather to Pandavas and Kouravas. He is called Veda Vyas because he had split the original version of Vedas into four parts; Veda Vyas literally means 'the splitter of Vedas'. It was because Veda

Vyasa had split the Vedas that it became easy for people to understand it. This is how divine knowledge was made available to everyone. It is still not clearly known whether Veda Vyas had split the Vedas all by himself or if he did with the help of a group of scholars.

In Mahabharata, Vyasa's mother marries the king of Hastinapur and gives birth to two sons. Both the sons die and their wives are left with no children. She asks him to impregnate both wives. He agrees. He tells these girls to come in close proximity to him but alone. It was Ambika's turn first to go close to him and out of shyness she closes her eyes and he declares that the baby would be born blind. This child was called Dhritarashtra. Then it was Amba's turn. Although she was instructed by Ambalika to relax and calm herself down. But she was nervous and her face became pale and Veda Vyas declared that the baby born will be severely anaemic and not be capable of running a kingdom. This was Pandu. It is said that Veda Vyasa asked Lord Ganesha himself to help in the compilation of Mahabharata. But Ganesha had put one condition on him, he said that he will write Mahabharata for him asking him to understand the verses even before he recited them. This is how Mahabharata was written. He also authored the Mahabharata.

Buddhism: In Buddhism, we find mention of Veda Vyasa. In the two of their Jataka tales called Kanha-dipayana and Ghata. He appeared as Bodhisattva in Kanha-dipayana and Ghata, which has no connection with his Hindu Vedic works and in Ghata Jakata his role has a close relation to Mahabharata. In Ghata, the vrishnis play a joke on Veda Vyas to test his powers.

<u>VALMIKI</u>

Born: India

Full name: Ratnakkardah

Parents: Charshani, Sumali

Religion: Hinduism

Notable work(s): Ramayana

Movement: Dharmic movement called Valmikism is based on Valmiki's teachings

The greatest poet India has ever had, the life history of Valmiki is a roller-coaster ride. He belonged to Hindu religion. His father's name was Pracheta. He was born as Agni Sharma to a Brahmin named Pracheta. The variations that this saint has had in life are beyond anyone's imagination. Born in the Naga, the details of Valmiki's life are not clear as there were no written records. He is the author of "Ramyana", one of the greatest epics of India. The Ramyana tells the story of prince Rama of Ayodhya who always struck to his morals and emerged triumphant in the battle fought with demon king Ravana. The biography of Valmiki is an intriguing one and the exact dates of existence doesn't known. Valmiki was not always a saint. He was an infamous bandit till his 30s. One day he was touched by an act of love between two birds and that transformed his personality drastically. He realized the power of speech he had in him and the ability to create rhythmic verses. He then had a divine vision of Brahma, who urged Valmiki to use this potential to the maximum and write the story of Ramayana. Thus began the preparation of one of the most sacred and revered epic of India. The poetry and language used in Ramyana are commendable and unmatched.

It is said that once Narada, a mythical sage, come to see Valmiki, and upon meeting him Valmiki asked him about an ideal man. Narada told him the story of Ramayana to answer his question. It was on this story that Valmiki built up his epic 24,000-versed poetry. Valmiki got so attached to the story recited by Narada that he left for river Tamasa along with his disciple Bharadwaj. He felt so peaceful and calm near the holy river that it helped him contemplate the modesty and maturity of his new-found hero. He witnessed a gruesome deed while he was feeling content and spiritual. A hunter killed a bird which was engrossed in a lover's play with its partner bird. This moved Valmiki beyond imagination. He felt a deep pang (emotional feeling or physical pain) in his heart. He witnesses such cruelty and got angry and cursed the hunter. He said to him in the form of a curse that nobody will ever respect him in society because he killed an innocent bird who was just involved in the act of love.He realized that he cursed him in the form of a 'sloka'. It was a metrical composition, perfect and rhythmic. This was defining movement of his life, he turned into a poet. It was a combination of all the respect and love he felt for Lord Rama and the tragedy he witnessed in the act of cruelty.

Major work: It is said that Valmiki taught Ramayana to the sons of Rama, Luv and Kush. He is also said to have given shelter to Sita after she was banished from the kingdom. The Ramayana is sung rather than first recited. Those who have read the Ramayana have bowed to Valmiki with great respect. It is said that when Luv and Kush were singing the Ramayana in their sweet voice in front of Rama, he himself was unaware of the fact that they were his own sons. Though the epic is still there, there are no written records of Valmiki and his period of existence. Valmiki has infact also got a small part in the actual Ramayana. When Rama along with his wife and brother is roaming around in exile in the jungle, Valmiki is one of the sages whom he visits on his way to Chitrakoot after leaving Ayodhya. Valmiki invites Rama, Sita and Laxman with lots of respect and love. He only says one word to Rama— 'Asyatam' which means please be seated. He feels very touched and honoured when Rama accepts his invitation and Sita with him for a while. There is another occasion where Valmiki had a little role to play. When Rama sends Sita into exile then Valmiki takes her in his shelter and keeps her and her two sons under his loving care. When there is an epic recitation of the poem takes place in the royal court. Rama insists on Valmiki to bring along Sita for her chastity test. This offends Valmiki an awful lot but he does not say anything and keeps mum. He goes along with the plan and persuades Sita to comply with her husband's wishes, even though internally he believed it to be a very wrong act from Rama's side. While Sita is made to take the chastity test by entering the fire pyre, Valmiki recites the pious words of penance and perseverance that he has practised all of his life just to help Sita prove her purity.

━━━━━ **CHAPTER-2** ━━━━━

2.1 INDIA'S STRUGGLE FOR FREEDOM: 1857 AS THE FIRST WAR OF INDEPENDENCE

The Mutiny of 1857 proved to be a landmark in the history of India. This Mutiny ended the company's rule. However, after the war the rule of the British Crown began. Not only common people took part in the Mutiny but also the princes, the Nawabs, the Rajas, the rulers, the Zamindars and even the Sepoys took interest in the Mutiny. During the Mutiny, the last Mughal Emperor Bahadur Shah Zafar (1837-1862) was proclaimed as the Emperor of India. The Mutiny began on 10th May 1857 and then spread like wildfire to different parts of the country. The people and the Sepoys rose to rebellion against the unlawful activities of the British government.

Introduction: The Revolt of 1857 was the first major challenge to the East India Company and literally put a comma to the colonial ambitions of its masters in England. During the Revolt, which took place in many parts of Central, Northern, and Eastern parts of India, different sections of society joined the rebel sepoys of the East India Company in what has been described by some scholars as the First War of Indian Independence.[23] It was on 10th May 1857 that the Mutiny began at Meerut. The Mutiny then spread to different parts of the country. The people from all our India proclaimed the last

Mughal Emperor Bahadur Shah Zafar as the Emperor of India. Different policies as devised by the Governor General Lord Wellesley (1798-1803) and the Governor General of India at that time i.e. Lord Dalhousie (1848-1856) had created unrest among the rulers and Nawabs of the princely states. Punjab, Sindh and Awadh were annexed under the policy of Subsidiary Alliance and Satara (1848), Sambalpur (1849), Jhansi (1854), Nagpur (1854) and Awadh (1856) were annexed under the policy of Doctrine of Lapse. Different historians had given their different views about the Mutiny of 1857. Some historians called it as Sepoy's Mutiny, some called it a war between the people of India and the British government because the Indians were insulted in every possible way by the British government. While some historians like Vinayak Damodar Savarkar commonly known as "Veer Savarkar" described it as the first war of independence because of the participation of not only sepoys but also of the people of India.

The outbreak and the Causes of the Mutiny: How did the Mutiny begin? What were the causes of the outbreak of the Mutiny? Why did the rulers, Nawabs, Rajas, common people including peasants, Zamindars and even the Sepoys rose to rebellion against the British and wanted to overthrow the rule of the British? The reason for this was the pitiless exploitation of the Indian people by the British. There are different causes which were responsible for the outbreak of the Mutiny of 1857. These are:

1. Immediate Cause: It was on 29th March 1857 that a young soldier Mangal Pandey of the 34th Native Infantry fired at his Senior Lieutenant Baugh at Barrackpur over the issue of newly greased cartridges which were thought to be greased with the pork (fats of pig) and beef (fats of cow). As cow was sacred to the Hindus and the pig was a taboo for the Muslims that's why Mangal Pandey opened fire at his senior. After this, there was widespread rumour among the sepoys about this hidden propaganda of the British thus, insulting the sepoys and the common people by hurting them on religious basis. Mangal Pandey was finally hanged on 8th April 1857. Later on, ninety men

                                    UNDERSTANDING HISTORY

of the 3rd Native Cavalry at Meerut refused to use such newly greased cartridges on 24th April 1857. The refusal resulted in the dismissal of eighty-five of them from their services who were also sentenced to 10 years confinement on 9th May 1857. The next morning i.e. on 10th May 1857, the Mutiny began at Meerut and the sepoys started their movement towards Delhi where they proclaimed the last Mughal Emperor Bahadur Shah Zafar as their Shahenshah-i-Hindustan or the Emperor of India. When the rebel sepoys raised the banner of revolt against the Raj, after decades of discontentment against the colonial policies of the British, the Rajas were shocked. They set out to help the Raj in suppressing the revolt with an iron hand. The company officials, who might have fled to their native country, if the revolt had succeeded in overthrowing the company rule, acted fast in acknowledging the favour and support of these Rajas. Even the appeal of Bahadur Shah Zafar went in vain. Bahadur Shah Zafar in his address to Indian Rajas said on May 20, 1857: "All you Rajas are famed for your virtues, noble qualities and liberality, and are moreover the protectors of your own faith and of the faith others. It is incumbent therefore on such of you as have the power to kill those who may injure your religion...and thus protect your faith..."[24]

2. Political Cause: The British followed the policy of expansion by introducing the policy of Doctrine of Lapse also known as Annexation Policy. This policy was devised by Governor General Lord Dalhousie (1848-1856). According to this policy, any ruler who died without a direct heir or who is weak and not able to rule, then his/her territory would automatically be annexed according to this annexation policy. The ruler also could not adopt a son if they had no direct heir. This created fear in the minds of other ruling families. Rani Lakshmi Bai's adopted son was not permitted to sit on the throne of Jhansi. Satara, Nagpur and Jhansi were annexed under the Doctrine of Lapse. Jaitpur, Sambalpur and Udaipur were also annexed. Other rulers feared that the annexation of their states was only a matter of time. The refusal to continue the pension of Nana Saheb, the adopted son of Baji

Rao II, created hostility among the ruling class.[25] By doing so, the British government hurt the sentiments of the Indian people. They felt broken because they were rendered jobless, hopeless, helpless etc. which results in discontentment among different sections of society against the British government.

3. Social cause: During the revolt of 1857, the Indian people were outraged because of the rapid spread of western civilization in India. People belonging to different class of society were treated very poorly. They had to work and fight for the British government, despite the low salaries and interference with the customs and traditions of the Indian people which made them realise that the British government was going to devastate the culture of the people of India. This aroused the feeling of discontentment among the people against the British government.

4. Religious cause: Another cause for the outbreak of the mutiny of 1857 was the passing of an Act in the year 1850 which changed the Hindu law of inheritance. According to this, a Hindu who had converted to Christianity can inherit the property of their ancestors. Other sources provide us with information about the Christian missionaries which were started by the British government in order to convert every Indian into Christianity which was totally against the religion of both Hindus and Muslims. Besides, the government's interference with the religion of both these communities hurt the sentiments of Indian people. Interference with certain prevailing laws like the Abolition of Sati, female infanticide and permitting widows to remarry and legalizing such laws were great threats to the whole society in India at that time and that's why the Indian people felt hurt because of passing and legalizing such laws and so people were outraged and turned against the British government and decided to free themselves from their rule.

5. Economic cause: The economic condition of the people of India during 1857 was not good. The heavy taxation and the discriminatory tariff policies had given a tough blow to the Indian people including peasants, artisans, zamindars etc. all of which were affected badly because of the destruction of handicrafts. In rural areas, peasants and zamindars resented the heavy taxes on land and the stringent methods of revenue collection followed by the Company. Many among these groups were unable to meet the heavy revenue demands and repay their loans to money lenders, eventually losing the lands that they had held for generations.[26] The people who were not able to repay their loans or those who were not able to give such taxes which were imposed by the British government were rendered hopeless, helpless and jobless, and remained unemployed for the most part of the year and died of poverty and starvation. Besides this, their landed property was also confiscated by the British which created a feeling of discontentment among the people of India and so they turned against the British government which in turn led to the outbreak of the Mutiny of 1857.

6. Military cause: The Mutiny of 1857 according to some historians started as a Sepoy Mutiny. However, later on people belonging to different classes of society also took part in the Mutiny. The Indian sepoys worked for the British and fought for them in distant areas leaving their own families back in villages. The sepoys were also given very low salaries. Indian sepoys formed more than 87% of British troops in India. They were considered inferior to British soldiers. An Indian sepoy was paid less than a European sepoy of the same rank. Besides, an Indian sepoy could not rise to a rank higher than that of a Subedar.[27] In 1856, the then Governor General Lord Canning (1856-1862) who later on become the first viceroy of India after the passage of Government of India Act 1858 passed and issued the General Services Enlistment Act. According to which the Indian sepoys were required to serve in distant areas even in British land across the sea. After the annexation of Awadh under the policy of Doctrine of Lapse by Lord Dalhousie (1848-1856), the army of Nawab of Awadh was disbanded. The sepoys lost their means of livelihood as they were left with no other source of income for their families which made them bitter enemies of the British and in this way the sepoys rose to rebellion against the British thus, raising the banner of revolt in the form of Sepoy Mutiny against the British.

DIFFERENT LEADERS FROM DIFFERENT REGIONS WHO WERE ASSOCIATED WITH THE MUTINY OF 1857

S.NO.	Name of the Region	Name of the Leader
1.	Barrackpore 34th Native Infantry	Mangal Pandey
2.	Bareilly	Bahadur Khan
3.	Bihar (Jagdishpur)	Amar Singh, Kunwar Singh (right known as Lion of Bihar)
4.	Delhi	General Bakht Khan, Bahadur Shah Zafar (The last Mughal Emperor)
5.	Faizabad	Maulvi Ahmadullah (The best soldier among the rebels)
6.	Jhansi	Rani Lakshmi Bai (Also known as Manu or Chhabelli)
7.	Kanpur/Gwalior	Nana Saheb (Actual name was Dondhu Alias Pant), Tantia Tope (Actual name was Ramchandra Pandu Ranga)
8.	Lucknow	(The capital of Awadh) Begum Hazrat Mahal and her son Birjish Qadar

Main Centres of the Mutiny: The Mutiny began at Meerut on 9th May 1857 and this day marked the beginning of the revolt of 1857. The Indian sepoys fought heroically and slaughtered their British officers and finally on 10th May 1857 they marched towards Delhi. The main centres from where the leaders revolted are given below:

1. **Delhi:** The Indian sepoys from different regions came out and joined with other sepoys in Delhi and the whole city came under their control. The next morning i.e., on 11th May 1857, they proclaimed Bahadur Shah Zafar as the Emperor of Hindustan.

2. **Lucknow:** At Lucknow the revolt was led by Begum Hazrat Mahal, the widow of Nawab Wajid Ali Shah. Lucknow was the capital of Awadh from where she revolted. At last, the British forces defeated her, and Begum Hazrat Mahal escaped to Nepal.

3. **Kanpur:** Here the revolt was led by Nana Saheb. Also known as Dondhu Alias Pant. He was the adopted son of Peshwa Baji Rao II. He led the revolt as he was refused to pension by the British government.

4. **Jhansi:** Here the revolt was led by Rani Lakshmi Bai, the wife of Raja Gangadhar Rao. She was defending her territory which Sir Hugh Rose wanted to annex under the policy of Doctrine of Lapse. She fought bravely but unfortunately; she died while fighting at Kalpi near Jhansi. Sir Hugh Rose who defeated her paid high tribute to her while saying that "Here lay the woman who was the only man among the rebels."

5. **Bihar:** Here the revolt was led by Kunwar Singh. He was a leading Rajput zamindar of Jagdishpur (Bihar). He was rightly regarded as the "Lion of Bihar." He was even rated as the most brilliant military strategist of the Mutiny of 1857.

6. **Faizabad:** The revolt was led by Maulvi Ahmadullah. He raised the banner of revolt at Faizabad. He was recognised even by the English, as a man of great abilities of great courage and stern determination and one of the best soldiers among rebels.

7. **Bareilly:** At Bareilly, the revolt was led by Khan Bahadur Khan. He raised his voice against the British. At last, he was captured treacherously, thereafter tried and finally hanged.

Suppression of the Mutiny of 1857:

1. Delhi was suppressed by John Nicholson and Lieutenant Hudson on 20th September 1857.

2. Lucknow was suppressed by Henry Lawrence, Henry Havelock, Sir Colin Campbell and James Outram on 21st March 1858.

3. Kanpur was suppressed by Sir Colin Campbell and Sir Hugh wheeler.

4. Jhansi was suppressed by Sir Hugh Rose on 17th June 1858.

5. Banaras was suppressed by Colonel James Neill.

Causes liable for the failure the Mutiny of 1857: Following are the causes which were responsible for the failure of the Mutiny of 1857. These are:

1. During the revolt the rebels were not united. In some places they fought against the British while at some other places, some rebels were in favour of British government only because they had been benefitted from the British government.

2. People from all over India did not take part in the Mutiny. They thought that their participation would affect their families if they failed to crush British government later.

3. There was no common motive among the Indian people for crushing the rebellion.

4. The military weapons of Indian sepoys were not superior in comparison with the British that's why the sepoys had to face defeat at many places.

5. The treacherous people like the rich merchants, traders, big zamindars etc. Provided full assistance to the British government to suppress the Mutiny. Although the revolt was widespread, a large part of the country remained unaffected by it. The revolt was mainly confined to the Doab region. Sind Rajputana, Kashmir, and most parts of Punjab. The southern provinces did not take part in it. It failed to have the character of an all-India struggle. Important rulers like Sindhia, Holkar, Rana of Jodhpur and others did not support the rebels.[28]

Outcome of the mutiny of 1857: The Mutiny of 1857 was a great challenge to the British by the Indian Sepoys. This revolt ended the rule of the East India Company, and the power was completely transferred to the British crown according to the Government of India Act 1858. The great uprising of 1857 was an important landmark in the history of modern India. The revolt marked the end of the East India Company's rule in India. India now came under the direct rule of the British Crown. This was announced by Lord Canning at a Durbar in Allahabad in a proclamation issued on 1st November 1858 in the name of the Queen.[29] Queen Victoria now took the charge of whole administration in her hands. She promised to every Indian whether Rajas, Rulers or Nawabs also they could now regain their old influence and privileges. Besides this, all the civil as well as military posts shall be given to them also if they would qualify to do so. The Government of India Act 1858 made the change in the designation of Governor General's office. Lord Canning (1856-1862) was now the last Governor General and had become the first viceroy of India. The annexation policy of Lord Dalhousie (1848-1856) was abrogated. Rulers could now regain their old privileges. The adoption of a son by any ruler or Nawab was now conceded. This revolt finally ended after suppression by some British officers and after making some provisions in the Government of India Act 1858 which benefitted Indians the most.

Conclusion: From the above discussion, it is concluded that the Mutiny of 1857 posed a serious threat to the British government. Not only sepoys but also the Rajas, Maharajas, rulers of princely states, Nawabs, peasants, Zamindars and the common people also participated in the mutiny because everyone has some own cause behind the bitterness against the British government. The earlier attempt to introduce reform and interfere with existing customs and traditions was discontinued. The viceroy informed the Maharajas and the Jagirdars (landlords) that in consideration of their loyalty to the

British government, in the event of failure of anyone of them of direct heirs, recognise the privilege of adoption, according to the ancient customs of their respecting families.[30] Lord Canning (1856-1862) after becoming the first Viceroy of India was aware of the situation, chaos and confusion which was prevalent there at that time. The Indians had already become the worst enemies of the British and had caused much more destruction everywhere. So, he (Canning) thought of not interfering with the customs and traditions of the people which compel the British to face heavy loss. Lord Canning thus made it clear that the rulers could now adopt a son onwards and there would be no annexation of any territory from this time onwards. The Government of India Act 1858 made some provisions in the interests of the Indians who revolted against the British in 1857. At last, it is not possible to say that whether it was a Sepoy Mutiny or people rebellion or any other view which had been put forwarded by different historians because not only sepoys but also different classes of the society including rulers, Nawabs, Maharajas, peasants, Zamindars whether Hindus or Muslims all of them were a part of this insurgency having their own different causes indulge them to be a part of this Mutiny. In a proclamation to the Princes Chiefs, and people of India, delivered November 1858 Queen Victoria (1837-1901) pledged to "respect the rights, dignity, and honour of native princes as our own". And guarantee that the policy of annexing princely states has come to an end.[31] Finally, the Mutiny came to an end after suppression and promises made by Queen Victoria.

GLOSSARY:

1. **Awadh:** Region in Central North India.

2. **Begum:** A title given to the wives of Muslim princes.

3. **Raja:** King.

4. **Maharaja:** Great king.

5. **Nawab:** Equivalent to Raja.

6. **Sepoy:** Soldier

2.2 IMPORTANT HEROES OF FREEDOM STRUGGLE, BIRSA MUNDA, BHAGAT SINGH, CHANDRA SHEKHAR AZAD, SUBASH CHANDRA BOSE

India got independence only because of the struggles and sacrifices of some great heroes who fought bravely againt the oppressive rule of the Britishers. They made every possible effort to overthrow them and free the Indians from their unjust and tyrannical rule. The independence movement of India would not have been possible without the contributions of such great freedom fighters. Some of the freedom fighters were Birsa Munda, Bhagat Singh, Chandra Shekhar Azad, Subhash Chandra Bose etc. Besides, these freedom fighters there were other freedom fighters also like Mahatma Gandhi, Jawahar Lal Nehru and others who also sacrificed their lives only for India's independence.

<u>BIRSA MUNDA</u>

Birsa Munda was a freedom fighter, religious leader and folk hero who belonged to the Munda tribe of Jharkhand. He is the unsung hero of India who took active participation in the freedom struggle of India. Birsa Munda is well-known for leading a tribal revolt against the British authorities in the Jharkhand region in the late 19th century. His achievements are even more remarkable for having been accomplished before the age of 25.

Early life: Birsa was born on 15 November 1875 in the village of Ulihatu in the Lohardaga district of Bengal Presidency, now in Khunti district of Jharkhand. Birsa's early life or years were spent with his parents at Chalkad. His early life could not have been very different from that of an average Munda child. He grew up grazing sheep, playing the flute, dancing in the local akharas etc.

Driven by poverty Birsa was taken to Ayubhatu, his maternal's uncle village. There he lived for two years he went to school at Salga, run by Jaipal Nag. He came in contact with a Christian missionary who visited a few families in the village which had been converted to Christianity.

Birsa Munda understood very soon that Christian missionaries were converting tribals to Christianity. Birsa soon started to challenge the Christian missionaries and revolted against the conversion activities along with the Munda and Oraon communities. Birsa is credited for reviving the traditional tribal culture which was mostly affected by Christian missionary work. Many tribals under his sect had already converted to Christianity. He opposed and criticised the church and its practices such as levying of taxes and religious practices. He himself became a preacher and a representative of their traditional tribal religion, and soon, he built up a reputation as a healer, a miracle worker, and a preacher. Birsa Munda started to advise tribal people to pursue their original traditional tribals religious system. Impressed by his teachings, he became a saintly figure to the tribal and they sought his blessings.

Tribal Movement: Birsa Munda's slogan threatening the British Raj: "Abu raj etc jana, maharani raj tundu jana" (let the kingdom of the queen be ended and our kingdom in the establishment) is still remembered in areas of Jharkhand, Odisha, Bihar, West Bengal and Madhya Pradesh. The life history of Birsa Munda will go down in the history of the tribals as a story of the emancipation of his own people, who were being suppressed by the Britishers. He was a visionary. He realized that the Britishers have come to this land to torture the masses and carry the wealth abroad.

The British colonial system intensified or decided to make the transformation of the tribal agrarian system into a feudal state. The tribals were also suppressed for long by Dikus (non-tribals) and intermediaries like Jhikadars and money lenders including zamindars who tried to exploit the tribals constantly. In some villages, they had completely lost their proprietary rights and had been reduced to the position of farm labourers. To the twin challenges of agrarian breakdown and culture change, Birsa along with the Munda responded through a series of revolts and uprisings under his leadership. In 1985 in Chalkad village of Tamar, Birsa renounced Christianity and asked his fellow tribesmen to worship only one God and giveup the worship of Bonqas. He said that the reign of Queen Victoria was over, and the Munda raj has begun. He gave orders to raiyats to pay no rent. The Munda called him Dharti Baba, the father of earth. Due to rumour that those who didn't follow Birsa would be massacred, Birsa was arrested on 24 Aug. 1895 and sentenced to two-year imprisonment. On 28 jun. 1898, after being released from jail he went with his followers and started war against British. For two years, they attacked places loyal to the British. On 5 Jan. 1900 Birsa's followers killed two police constable at Etkodid. On 7 Jan. they attacked the Khanty police station, killing a constable and razing the house of a local shopkeeper. The local commissioner, A. Fober, and deputy commissioner, H.C. Streatfield, rushed to Khanty with a force of 150 men to suppress growing rebellion. The colonial administrator also set a reward of Rs 500 for capturing Birsa. The troops under the command defeated Munda's guerrillas at Dumbari Hill, though Munda himself escaped to the Singhbum hills. He was arrested at Jamkopai forest in Chakradharpur on 3 February 1900. According to deputy commissioner Ranchi, Vide Letter, 460 tribals were made accused in 15 different cases, but of which 53 were convicted. Birsa Munda died in jail in June 1900, and it is also believed that he died due to cholera. After his death, the movement faded out. In 1908 the colonial government introduced the Chotanagpur Tenancy Act which prohibits the transfer of tribal land to non-tribals.

The birth anniversary of the iconic tribal leader like Birsa Munda is observed as Janjatiya Gaurav Divas by the Modi government on Nov. 15 every year.

BHAGAT SINGH

Bhagat Singh was one of the prominent heroes of the freedom struggle who sacrificed his life happily for the sake of his country. His heart was soaked in patriotism since childhood. He brought a revolution in the national movement against the British rule. He was a prominent freedom fighter and he inspired the youth to join him in fight against the British rule.

Early Childhood: Bhagat Singh was born on September 28, 1907, in the district of Lyallpur in Punjab which is now in Pakistan. He was the third son of Sardar Kishan who was a revolutionary himself and Vidywati. His father was in jail when Bhagat Singh was born. He was a very good student. It is said that when he was young he was very friendly by nature. Bhagat Singh attended Dayanand Vedic School and National College both located in Lahore. He was against the British rule in India and he began to protest for national independence. In 1928 Bhagat Singh made a plan with others to kill a police chief who was responsible for the killing of Indian writer and politician Lala Lajpat Rai popularly known as Lion of Punjab during the Anti-Simon Comission on 17th Nov. 1928.

Upon being asked what he wanted to be when he grew up, he said he would drive the British out of India. He was very much disturbed by the incident of Jallianwala Bagh tragedy in the year 1919. He was only twelve years old then and the incident left a very deep scar in his heart. He brought home a bottle of mud-soaked in the blood of the victims and worshipped it. He was always attracted to socialism and he set his path for political revolutionaries, which no one even thought of as he wanted to overthrow the Britishers. He was clear in his vision and he dedicated himself to achieving his goals. He left his school and he took part in the Congress Movement. He actively supported the Swadeshi Movement i.e. use of Swadeshi goods and the boycott of foreign goods. He decided to wear only Khadi Clothes. He supported Swadeshi Movement where a bonfire of foreign clothes was started at various places. In Maharashtra the movement was led by Bal Gangadhar Tilak popularly known as "Lokmanya".

His Struggle for Freedom: After the Chauri Chaura incident where violent mob killed 22 policemen, Gandhi Ji withdrew his Movement as his faith in people to follow non-violence weakened. He started believing that the only way to overthrow the British out of the country would be through armed rebellion. He studied the lives of the revolutionaries of Ireland, Italy and Russia and was convinced of

 UNDERSTANDING HISTORY

his belief. He joined National College, which was patronized by great patriots like Lala LajpatRai. In the daytime, he would attend classes and in the evening he would discuss the revolution with his friends. He contacted the leader of Bengal Revolutionary Party, Sachindranath Sanyal, the author of " Bandi Jevan" to join his party. But he could join the party only onone condition which was that whenever required he should be ready to leave his home immediately. He reached Kanpur and there he started selling newspapers to earn a little bit for his survival. It is said that Ganesh Vidyarthi who was a revolutionary offered him a job at his periodical office. He supported Akali Dal's meetings. He went to Lahore and became secretary of Naujawan Bharat Sabha.

He was arrested as police suspected his hand in the Dussehra bombing case. He was bailed out by two wealthy men. After running his father's diary for a while, he left for Delhi. Bhagat Singh believed only in revolution to win freedom and so he joined Chandra Shekhar Azad. He shaved his beard and kept short-cropped hair.

Thereafter, he learnt to make bombs from Jatin Das in Kolkata. In Agra, they setup a bomb factory. They continued with their activities even though they did not have enough money to eat.

Turning Point in His Life: In 1928, when Lala Lajpat Rai died in a Lathi charge, Bhagat Singh along with Rajguru shot John Saunders, mistaking him for Scott, the police officer to avenge his death. In 1929, he and Bakuteshwar Dutt exploded a bomb at the Legislative Assembly Hall in Delhi and shouted slogans of "Inquilab Zindabad" but they did not intend to hurt or kill anyone but to express their disagreement with the ordinance of Defense of Indian Act that was to be formulated. They surrendered themselves and they were sentenced to 116 days in jail.

In the jail, he witnessed discrimination between the European and Indian prisoners and led other prisoners on a hunger strike to protest against this. They demanded equality in food standards, clothing, etc. After a month's strike, the British were forced to agree to their demands.

Finally, Bhagat Singh, Sukhdev and Rajguru were convicted of assassinating John Saunders and exploding two bombs at the Legislative Assembly Hall and the order of death sentence on 24th March 1931 was passed. But the schedule was preponed and they were hanged on 23rd March 1931 at 7:30 pm in the Lahore jail.

Even on the fateful day, they were fearless and competed with each other to be hanged first. While getting hanged, they chanted 'Bharat Mata ki Jai'. This is how the fearless revolutionaries sacrificed their lives for the sake of their motherland.

That day, none of the prisoners ate food. Their bodies were secretly cremated on the banks of Sutlej.

Conclusion: Even today, Bhagat Singh is remembered for his dauntless spirit. He was the source of inspiration for the youth of the nation. His sacrifice and his dedication to free his country from the British would be engraved in the golden words in the history of the freedom struggle. The title 'Shaheed' was awarded to him for his fearless contribution towards freedom.

CHANDRA SHEKHAR AZAD

Chandra Shekhar Tiwari who was popularly known as Chandra Shekhar Azad. He was an Indian revolutionary leader and a freedom fighter. His birthplace is in present-day Alirajpur district of Madhya Pradesh. He belonged to a poor family. His father's name was Sitaram Tiwari and his mother's name was Jagrani Devi. He received his education at Bhavra and later went to Kashi Vidyapeeth Banaras for higher education. At a very young age, he involved himself in revolutionary activities. It was in the year 1921 when he joined the Non-cooperation Movement which was started by Mahatma Gandhi to protest against the Jallianwala Bagh Massacre. At the age of 15, he was imprisoned for the first time when he was captured by the Britishers. After this incident, he took the surname "Azad" and came to be known as Chandra Shekhar Azad.

Revolutionary Activities of Chandra Shekhar Azad: The suspension of Non-cooperation Movement in Feb. 1922 due to the Chauri Chaura incident gave a blow to Azad's nationalist sentiments. During this time he met with many young revolutionary leaders of India like Ram Prasad Bismil, Jogesh Chandra Chatterji, Sachindra Nath Sanyal, Sachindra Nath Bakshi and Ashfaqullah Khan who formed Hindustan Republican Association (HRA) in 1923. He then became a member of Hindustan Republican Association and later on he along with prominent leaders like Roshan Singh, Rajendra Lehri and Ashfaqullah Khan reorganized the Hindustan Republican Association under the new name of Hindustan Socialist Republican Association. He was involved in the Kakori train robbery in 1925. He shot J.P. Saunders to avenge Lala Lajpat Rai's murder who was killed during Anti-Simon Commission in the year 1928. Azad made Jhansi the headquarter of his Hindustan Republican Association.

Chandra Shekhar Azad's Death: Chandra Shekhar Azad shot himself when he was surrounded by the police at Alfred Park which is now famously known as Azad Park in Allahabad on February 27, 1931. After this incident, his body was taken to Rasulabad Ghar for cremation without telling the general public. People crowded the park where this incident took place and chanted anti-British slogans and thanked Azad.

Famous Quotes of Chandra Shekhar Azad: Some of the famous slogans of Chandra Shekhar Azad were as follows:

- *Aisi Jawani kisi kaam ki Nahi jo apni Matra Bhoomi ke Kaam Na aa sake.*

- *I believe in a religion that propagates freedom, equality and brotherhood.*

NETAJI SUBHASH CHANDRA BOSE

His contribution to the Indian freedom struggle: Netaji Subhash Chandra Bose was born on 23rd January 1897 in Cuttack, Orissa. His father's name was Janki Nath Bose and his mother's name was Prabhavati Devi. His father was a famous lawyer. Netaji was a great Indian nationalist leader who fought with great courage, during the second world war for the independence of India against the British rule.

Netaji was a revolutionary freedom fighter of India. Subhash Chandra Bose was one of the greatest men and brave freedom fighter in Indian history. His great contribution to the freedom struggle in the history of India is unforgettable. Netaji always believed in violence. He passed the B.A. (Honours in Philosophy) examination in 1918 with first division. He was awarded second position in University of Calcutta. His parents sent him to the University of Cambridge in England to prepare for Indian Civil Services (ICS) examination. In the year 1920, he passed the ICS examination, but on hearing about the Jallianwala Bagh massacre he quit his high-paying ICS job and came back to India from England in 1921 to join India's struggle for independence. Soon, he left home to become an active member of India's independent movement and joined the Indian National Congress.

Subhash Chandra Bose and Congress: On returning to India, he came under the influence of Mahatma Gandhi. He joined Non-cooperation movement started by Gandhi to make INC a powerful non-violent organization. During the movement he was advised by M.K. Gandhi to work with Chittranjan Das who became his political guru. While Chittranjan Das was busy in developing a national strategy. Subhash Chandra Bose played a crucial role in enlightening the students, youths and labourers of Calcutta. He was eager and waiting to see India independent, federal and republic nation. He started the newspaper 'Swaraj' in 1921. In 1924 he became the CEO of Calcutta Municipal Corporation. Bose was sent to prison in Mandalay for nationalist activities in 1925. In 1927 he was released from prison and was elected the president of All India Youth Congress and also the secretary of the Bengal state. In 1930, he became the mayor of Calcutta. Bose authored the book "The Indian struggle" which covers the Indian independence movement from 1920-24. The book was banned by the

British government. In 1938 he was elected as president of the Indian National Congress and formed a national planning committee, which formulated a policy of broad industrialization.

An important development in the struggle for freedom during the second world war was the formation and activities of the Azad Hind Fauj, also known as the Indian National Army or INA in 1943 which was initially formed in 1942 by Rash Behari Bose. The assault by the INA, no matter how short-lived it was, was an important factor that eventually contributed to the British decision to stop their operations and shift back to their own land. This in the end, did pave the way for India's Independence.

Although it was believed that Netaji Subash Chandra Bose died in a plane crash, his body was never recovered. There have been many theories put forward regarding his disappearance. The government of India set up a number of committees to investigate the case and come out with the truth. The Figgess Report 1946 and the Shah Nawaz Committee 1956 concluded that Bose died in a plane crash in Taiwan. The Kholsa Commission 1970 concluded that Bose died as concurred in the previous report.

Subhash Chandra Bose, a great personality and a great adventurer, played a crucial role in freeing the country from the clutches of 200 years of British rule in his own inimitable way much like the other leading lights of the day such as Mahatma Gandhi and Jawahar Lal Nehru. To commemorate his contribution to India's struggle for independence, every year on 23rd January, Subhas Chandra Bose's birthday is celebrated across various parts of the country. He was sent to prison 11 times during 1920-41. Till the last day of his life as an active freedom fighter, he kept the spirit of fighting against the British, and it is his persistence and patriotic favour that needs to respected more than anything else.

"It is our duty to pay for our liberty with our own blood. The freedom that we shall win through our sacrifice and exertions, we shall be able to preserve with our own struggle."

2.3 FORMATION OF INDIAN NATIONAL CONGRESS AND CONTRIBUTION OF MAHATMA GANDHI; MAKING OF INDIAN CONSTITUTION AND ITS SALIENT FEATURES

Introduction: Since the 1870s, the measures taken by British, rulers in India strengthens the political aspiration of Indians. The political organisation that emerged in the later 1870s and early 1880s were more critical of the British rulers and demanded more rights from the government. Thus, a solid ground had been prepared for the establishment of an all India organisation.

Formation of Indian National Congress: He was a retired English civil servant, A.O. Hume, who led the foundation of the Indian National Congress. He organised the first session of the Indian National Congress at Gokuldas Tejpal Sanskrit College in Bombay in December 1885 which was presided over by Womesh Chandra Banerjee, the first President of Indian National Congress. As a prelude to this, two sessions of the Indian National Congress had been held in 1883 and 1885, which had representatives from all major towns of India. Surendranath Banerjee and Ananda Mohan Bose were the main architects of the Indian National conference.

The first session of the Indian National Congress was attended by 72 delegates and this Session was Ist presided over by Womesh chandra Banerjee. There were 54 Hindus, 2 Muslims and the remaining members were Jain and Parsi. Hereafter, Congress met every year in December in different parts of the country each time. Some of the important leaders of the congress during this early period were Dadabhai Naroji, Badruddin Tayyab ji, Pheroz Shah Mehta, P. Anandacharlu, Surendra Nath Banerjee, Bal Gangadhar Tilak, Romesh Chandra Dutta, Ananda Mohan Bose and Gopal Krishna Gokhale. Other prominent leaders included Mahadev Govind Ranade, Bal, Sisir Kumar Ghosh, Motilal Ghosh, Madan Mohan Malaviya etc.

In 1890, Kadambini Ganguly, the first women graduate of Calcutta University, addressed the Indian National Congress.

FOLLOWING PRESIDENTS PRESIDED OVER THE DIFFERENT SESSIONS AT DIFFERENT TIMES OF THE YEAR:

S. No.	President Name	Year	Session
1.	Womesh Chndra Banerjee	1885	Bombay
2.	Dada Bhai Naroji	1886	Calcutta
3.	Badruddin Tayyab ji (Ist Muslim President)	1887	Madras
4.	Rahimtullah M.Sayani	1896	Calcutta
5.	Dada Bhai Naroji	1906	Calcutta
6.	Ras Behari Ghosh	1907	Surat
7.	Bishan Narayan Dar	1911	Calcutta
8.	Ambica Charan Majumdar	1916	Lucknow
9.	Annie Besant	1917	Calcutta
10.	M.K. Gandhi	1924	Belgaon
11.	Jawahar Lal Nehru	1929	Lahore
12.	Sardar Vallabhbhai Patel	1931	Karachi
13.	Subhash Chandra Bose	1938	Haripura
14.	Subhash Chandra Bose	1939	Tripura
15.	Acharya J.B. Kriplani	1946	Meerut

Aims and Objectives of the INC:

The main aims of the Indian National Congress in the initial stages were:

- To initiate a democratic nationalist movement.
- To politicise and politically educate people.
- To establish the headquarters for a movement.
- To promote friendly relations among nationalist political workers from different parts of the country.

- To develop and propagate an anti-colonial nationalist ideology.

- To formulate and present popular demands before the government with a view to unifying the people over a common economic and political programme.

- Develop and consolidate a feeling of national unity among people irrespective of religion, caste or province.

- Carefully promote and nurture Indian nationhood.

Foundational Theories: Safety Value Theory (Lajpat Rai): The fact that the INC was founded by a retired civil servant A.O. Hume, rather than an Indian has led to speculation that A.O. Hume founded INC to provide a 'safety value' to the growing dissatisfaction with British rule.

I. It has also been reported that Hume received the idea for an annual conference of educated Indians for political discussion with Viceroy Dufferin.

II. It may be true in part, but there is no reliable evidence that Dufferin suggested the formation of INC or that the INC was intended as a 'safety value'.

Conspiracy theory R.P Dutt:

- The Marxist historians conspiracy theory accuse of the 'safety value' concept.

- According to R.P Dutt, the INC accuse of conspiracy to suppress a popular uprising in India and the middle-class leaders were complicit in it.

Lightning Conductor Theory (G.K. Gokhale): It was presented by Gopal Krishna Gokhale. As per theory nationalists were aware of A.O. Hume's status as an enlightened imperialist. They were all aware that A.O. Hume intended to use them for the protection of the British empire.

FEATURES:

- The Indian leaders understood that if pan-India platform was established under the leadership of some Indian nationalists, the British would not allow it to survive.

- They wanted to keep A.O. Hume in the lead because he was white and British. As a result, congress was shielded by the British depression.

- Gokhale explains the need for an English founder of INC using lightning conductor theory.

- According to Indian modern Indian historians the Indian National congress represented the desire of politically conscious Indians to establish a national body to express the Indians political and economic demands.

- The early congress leaders used Hume as a lightning conductor that is, as a catalyst to bring together nationalist forces, even if it was disguised as a 'safety value'.

- Gopal Krishna Gokhale was a firm believer in the lightning conductor theory.

Gandhi and the Indian National Congress or the Contribution of Mahatma Gandhi:

Mahatma Gandhi was born on 2nd October 1869 at Porbandar in Gujarat. His full name was Mohan Das Karam Chand Gandhi. Gopal Krishna Gokhale was the Political Guru of Mahatma Gandhi. He was called the 'Father of the Nation' by Subhash Chandra Bose. He played an important role during India's freedom struggle.

Mahatma Gandhi is known to have entered and quickly risen in the Indian political scenario following his return from South Africa in 1915. He emerged as a guiding light with a breath of fresh air in the Indian National Congress which at the time was dominated by the combative policies of the extremists. Bal Gangadhar Tilak,

Lala Lajpat Rai and Bipin Chandra were the chief propagators of these extremist tendencies within the ranks of the INC. Gandhi's modes and ideologies were markedly different and were slow to gain acceptance.

However, he soon became a member of INC and then engaged in a nationwide journey under the command and wish of Sri Gopal Krishna Gokhale, his political mentor.

Mahatma Gandhi as the President of Indian National Congress: Mahatma Gandhi was elected as the president of the Indian National Congress in 1921. He immediately introduces several reforms within the party ranks. The responsibility Gandhi undertook as the president of INC was to increase the reach of the party among the masses who reside in the remote corners to eradicate aristocratic status.

Gandhi famously stated that rural India was the very backbone of the country, both in economic and logistical terms. Therefore, no movement can be truly successful unless whole-heartedly supported by the inhabitants of the Indian villages. The first step that he took was to insuperably reduce the membership fee of the party. Then he reconstructed the entire party hierarchy and opened new party branches in various provinces and princely states of India. Soon congress took a national dimension with membership multiplied manifold. Gandhi became the new guiding star of Indian politics, operating under the umbrella of the Indian National Congress.

As a president of the INC, Mahatma Gandhi introduced the tenets and the ideals of satyagraha, and the party saw the emergence of many new and charismatic leaders with great public appeals, who were loyal followers of Gandhi. By then, Lala Lajpat Rai also became an admirer of Gandhi despite their former differences. With such great following, non-cooperation movement against the Rowlatt Act and the Amritsar tragedy naturally took a massive national dimension.

MAKING OF THE INDIAN CONSTITUTION

Introduction: Constitution is defined as a set of fundamental principles according to which a state organisation is governed. It took about 2 years, 11 months and 18 days, approximately 3 years to finalize our constitution. The idea to have the Constitution was first given by M.N. Roy. Our Constitution declares India as Sovereign, Socialist, Secular, Democratic and Republic.

In 1938, Indian Nation Congress declared that the Constitution of free India must be framed, without outside interference, by a constituent assembly (the idea of constituent assembly was put forward by M.N. Roy in 1934) elected based on adult franchise.

The demand of Constituent Assembly was accepted by the British Government. In 1946 finally Cabinet Mission (three members named Lord Pethick Lawrence, Sir Stafford Cripps and AV Alexander) was sent and they arrived in India on 24th March, 1946.

The Constituent Assembly:

(a) The Constituent Assembly was constituted in November 1946 under the scheme formulated by the cabinet Mission Plan. The Constituent Assembly's total strength was 389. Of these 296 seats were to be allotted to British India and 93 to the princely states.

(b) The constituent Assembly held its first meeting on 9th December 1946. The meeting was attended by only 211 members. On 13th December 1946, Jawaharlal Nehru moved the historic objective resolution in the Assembly. It laid down the fundamentals and philosophy of constitutional structure.

(c) This resolution was unanimously adopted by the Assembly on 22nd January 1947. It influenced the eventual shaping of the constitution through all its subsequent stages. It modified versions of forms of the preamble of the present constitution.

(d) The last session of the Constituent Assembly was held on 24th January 1950.

Important Points to Remember:

- ☞ Dr. Sachidanand Sinha was the first temporary President of Constituent Assembly (9th December 1946).

- ☞ Dr. Rajendra Prasad was the first President of Constituent Assembly (11th December 1946).

- ☞ Objective Resolution was moved in the Constituent Assembly passed by Jawahar Lal Nehru (13th December 1946).

Enactment of the Constitution:

It took about 2 years, 11 months and 18 days to finalize our Constitution.

Dr. B.R. Ambedkar introduced the final draft of the constitution in the Assembly on 4th Nov. 1948. The constitution was enacted on 26th Nov. 1949 and contained a preamble, 395 Articles and 8 Schedules.

The remaining provisions of the constitution came into force on 26th January 1950. The day is referred to in the constitution as the 'Date of its Commencement' and celebrated as Republic Day.

Salient Features of the Indian Constitution:

The salient features of the Indian constitution, as it stands today are as follows:

(a) **Written Constitution:** In a federation, there should be a written constitution. The written constitution is very essential for a federal so that whenever there is any dispute between the federal government and federating units. It can be used as evidence.

(b) **Largest Constitution:** In sheer physical terms, our constitution is definitely the largest, bulkiest and most detailed constitution in the world. As originally passed, it contained 395 articles and 8 schedules. Presently it consists of a preamble, about 448+ Articles (divided into 25 parts) and 12 Schedules.

(c) **Sovereign, Democratic and Republic:** A sovereign nation is initially supreme and independent of any outside control. The word 'socialist' aims at the establishment of an egalitarian society in India. The term 'secular' means a state which has no official religion.

(d) **Parliamentary Type of Government:** In a parliamentary type of government, the head of the state is nominal, whereas the prime minister who is the leader of the majority in the parliament is the real executive. The Indian Constitution establishes in India a parliamentary type of government on the British model.

(e) **Partly Rigid and Partly Flexible:** There are certain provisions which can be amended by a simple majority in the parliament while there are certain provisions whose amendments require not any special majority in parliament, but also ratification by at least one-half of the state legislature.

(f) **Fundamental Rights:** Under the Indian Constitution as originally enacted, the citizen of India had been granted the seven fundamental rights (currently six). These rights are mentioned in Part III of the Constitution and are justifiable.

(g) **Fundamental Duties:** The 42nd constitutional amendment added a new part to the constitution i.e.., under the heading fundamental duties lays down a code of ten (currently eleven) duties for all the citizen of India.

(h) **Directive Principle of the State:** The concept of Directive Principle has been borrowed from the constitution of Ireland. These principles are contained in the part IV of the constitution. The aim of these principles is to establish a welfare state in India on the socialist pattern of society.

(i) **Independent judiciary:** The Indian constitution provides for an independent judiciary. The constitution made the supreme court the custodian and protector of the constitution. The judgements of the supreme court are legally binding and there is no appeal against the judgement of the supreme court.

(j) **A secure state:** Under the 42nd Amendment, the word 'secular' has been included in the preamble of the constitution. A secular state is one that does not consider anyone's religion as an official religion. It treats all its citizens equally, regardless of relgion. Thus, India has now become officially a secular state.

(k) **Single Citizenship:** The constitution of India grants one citizenship to all, sometimes citizens get double citizenship, one for the union and the other for the state in which a person lives.

(*l*) **Universal Adult Franchise:** The Indian constitution originally granted a universal adult franchise to all those men and women, who attained the age of 21 years. Under the 61st constitutional amendment the age of voting has been reduced from 21-18 years.

2.4 RE-EMERGENCE OF SWADESHI MOVEMENT IN INDIA; FLAGSHIP PROGRAMMES; JAN DHAN YOJANA; SKILL INDIA MISSION; MAKE IN INDIA; ATMA NIRBHAR BHARAT

Re-emergence of Swadeshi Movement in India: The Swadeshi movement was a self-sufficiency movement that was a part of the Indian independence movement and helped to shape Indian nationalism. The swadeshi movement began in 1905 as a unified reaction to Bengal's partition and lasted until 1908. It was, infact, the most successful of the pre-Gandhian movements. After the British government's decision was made public in 1903, there was widespread dissatisfaction among Indians. In response, the swadeshi movement was formally launched on August 7, 1905, from Town Hall, Calcutta, with the goal of reducing reliance on foreign goods in favour of domestic production.

Swadeshi Movement–Partition of Bengal:

- The partition of Bengal was the most significant event during Lord Curzon's reign. It was done primarily for administrative convenience. From 1899-1905 Lord Curzon was the viceroy of India.

- On October 16, 1905, the partition of Bengal province took place during his viceroyalty.

- Some people recognised Lord Curzon's true motivation and launched the anti-partition movement.

- They made the anti-partition movement not to be divided, and because this was the spirit of nationalism among Indians, they dubbed it the Swadeshi movement.

- The Swadeshi movement was a popular strategy for ending British rule and improving the country's economic condition.

Swadeshi Movement–Nature of the Movement:

- The Bengal leaders believed that demonstrations, public, and resolutions would have little impact on in the rulers.

- More positive action was required to reveal the intensity of popular feelings and display them at their best. Swadeshi and boycotts were the solutions.

- Swadeshi, or the use of Indian goods, and the boycott of British goods were declared and pledged at mass meetings held throughout Bengal.

- Public burnings of foreign cloth were organized in many places, and shops selling foreign cloth were picketed.

- The emphasis on self-reliance, or Atama Shakti, was an important aspect of the Swadeshi movement.

- National education was another self-sufficient, contented activity undertaken at the time.

The Extent of Mass Participation:

- Bengali students played an important role in the Swadeshi agitation. They practised and propagated Swadeshi and led picketing campaigns against shops selling foreign clothing.

- The government made every effort to silence the students. Orders were issued to penalize schools and colleges whose students participated actively in the Swadeshi agitation.

- The active participation of women in the Swadeshi agitation was a notable feature of the movement.

- Many prominent Muslims, including Abdul Rasul, a barrister, Liaquat Hussain, a well-known agitator and Guznavi, a businessman, joined the Swadeshi movement. Maulana Abdul Kalam Azad joined revolutionary terrorists.

Government Acts for Repressing Swadeshi Movement:

- Repressive measures were taken by the government. to suppress the Swadeshi and the Boycott Movement.

- The government banned holding of rallies, taking out processions, censored newspapers and imprisoned the leaders of the national movement.

- The government passed various Acts to curb the growth of movement:

    1. Seditious Meeting Act (1907).

    2. Criminal Law Amendment Act (1908).

    3. Indian Newspaper (Incitement to Offences) Act (1908).

    4. Explosive Substances Act (1910).

    5. Indian Press Act (1910).

Swadeshi Movement–Impact:

- It resulted in a significant decrease in imports from1905-1908.

- The movement resulted in the rise of extreme nationalism among young people, who turned to violence in order to put on and to British dominance.

- It compelled the British regime to make concessions to Indians in the form of Morley-Minto reforms in 1909 Gopal Krishna Gokhale was instrumental in developing these reforms.

- The National council of education was established in Aug. 1906 to organize the national education system. Bengal Institute of Technology was established to provide technical education.

- Foreign goods such as clothing, Sugar, Salt and other luxury items were not only boycotted, but also burned.

- The Swadeshi movement also resulted in a social boycott of both buyers and sellers of foreign goods.

Evaluation of the Swadeshi Movement: By 1908, the open phase of the Swadeshi and boycott movement was almost over. This was due to many reasons:

- There was severe government repression.

- The movement failed to create an effective organization or party structure. It throws up an entire gamut of techniques that later came to be associated with Gandhian politics, non-cooperation, passive resistance, filling of British jails, social reform, and constructive work but failed to give these techniques a disciplined focus.

○ The movement was unable to keep the masses enthralled.

○ The movement was unable to maintain the high pitch that it had achieved.

○ The Surat split in 1907 shattered the leadership's unity.

○ The movement's prominent leaders were arrested, leaving the movement without a leader.

FLAGSHIP PROGRAMMES

Jan Dhan Yojana: Pradhan Mantri Jan Dhan Yojana (PMJDY), one of the biggest financial inclusion initiatives in the world, was announced by prime-minister Shri Narendra Modi on 15th August from the ramparts of the Red Fort. (PMJDY) Pradhan Mantri Jan Dhan Yojna is a national mission for financial inclusion to ensure access to financial services, namely, banking (savings/deposits) accounts, remittance, credit, insurance, and pension in an affordable manner.

PRADHAN MANTRI JAN DHAN YOJANA

Features:

- Zero balance savings account can be opened with minimum documents.

- No mandate to maintain any minimum balance in these accounts.

- These accounts are like regular savings accounts and offer interest on the deposit.

- Accountholders also receive a Rupay debit card.

                              UNDERSTANDING HISTORY

- Accountholder can enrol for an accident insurance cover of Rs. 2 lakh (for accounts opened after 28-8-2018 and Rs. 1 lakh for accounts opened before this date).

- An overdraft facility of up to Rs 10,000 (only eligible accountholders).

- Receive benefits of government schemes such as Direct in Benefit Transfer (DBT), Mantri Jeevan Jyoti Beema Yojana (PMJJBY), Atal Pension Yojana (APY) and the Micro Units Development and Refinance Agency Bank (MODRA) scheme.

Objectives:

(a) Key objective of the PMJDY is to ensure access to financial services such as basic savings and deposits accounts, insurance, pension, credit and remittance to all households at an affordable cost.

(b) Basic bank account acts as a focal point of this scheme and the scheme started off by requesting all citizens (without any bank account) to open an account under PMJDY. Government reached out to all public and private banking providers to support the scheme and helps the citizens to open accounts in any branch.

(c) Creating a pull for opening bank accounts among the underserved population was a key challenge and to overcome this, the government focused on bottlenecks that restricted citizens from opening accounts. These bottlenecks include a long list of required documents, bank criteria of minimum balance in accounts and limited banking infrastructure availability.

(d) The government has developed policies for these bottlenecks which has resulted in higher adoption of the scheme and opening of new accounts.

Skill India Mission: Skill India Mission is a government scheme launched in 2015. It is an umbrella scheme that has many skilling schemes and programmes under it. The chief objective is to empower the youth of the country with adequate skill sets that will enable their employment in relevant sectors and also improve productivity.

Skill India Mission Latest update: Assam's chief minister Sarbananda Sonowal laid the foundation for first east India skills university in the Darrang district which aims to educate more than 10,000 students in 12 disciplines.

Skill India objectives:

(a) The chief objective of the skill India mission is to provide market-relevant skills training to more than 40 crore young people in the country by the year 2022.

(b) The mission intends to create opportunities and space for the development of talent in Indian youth.

(c) It aims to develop those fallers who have been put under skill development for the last many years, and also recognize new sectors for skill development.

Other Objectives are:

(a) Closing the gap between skill required by the industry and skill people possess for employment generation.

(b) Reducing poverty in country.

(c) Increasing the competitiveness of Indian business.

(d) Ensuring that skill training imparted is relevant and of equality.

(e) Diversifying the existing skill development programmes to meet today's challenge.

(f) Mobilising adequate investment for financing skills development sustainablity.

Features of Skill India:

(a) The focus is on improving the employability of the youth so that they get employment and enhances entrepreneurship among them.

(b) The mission offers training, guidance, and support for all traditional types of employment like weavers, cobblers, carpenters, welders, mansions, blacksmiths etc.

(c) New domains will be emphasised and such as real estate, transportation, construction, gem industry, textiles, banking, tourism, and other sectors where the level of skill is inadequate.

(d) Training imparted would be of international standards so that India's youth get jobs not only in India but also abroad where there is demand.

(e) An important feature is the creation of a new hallmark 'Rural India Skill'.

(f) Customised need-based programmes would be started for specific age groups in communication life, and positive thinking skills, language skills, behavioural skills, management skills etc.

(g) A course methodology would also not be unconventional and would be innovative. It would involve games, brainstorming sessions, group discussion, case studies and so on.

Sub-schemes under Skill India:

- National Skill Development Mission (NSDM).
- Pradhan Mantri Kaushal Vikas Yajna (PMKVY).
- Indian Skill development service.
- National policy for skill development and entrepreneurship 2015.
- Skill loan scheme.
- PM-YUVS Pradhan Mantri Yuva Udymita Vikas Abhiyan.

MAKE IN INDIA

Make in India program/government schemes: Launched in September 2014, the Make in India program is a government initiative focused on encouraging companies to manufacture in India. This government initiative which intends to boost the domestic manufacturing sector and augment foreign investment in the country. The make in India program is one of the key projects of the government intends to:

- Revive the hitherto lagging manufacturing sector of India to enhance the growth of the economy.

- Encourage foreign businesses to invest in India for their manufacturing needs.

- Improve India's rank in ease of doing business Index ease of doing business is a report published by the World Bank. It compares the business Regulation in 190 economics. In 2020, India's rank in the ease of doing business Index was 63.

- Develop India into a global manufacturing hub.

- And to boost employment opportunities in the country.

Sectors covered under make in India Program: Through the Make in India program, the government is focused on creating jobs and launching skill development programmes in some of the key sectors. These sectors include:

- Manufacturing sectors:

- Aerospace and defence.

- Automotive and auto components.

- Biotechnology.

- Capital goods.

- Textile and apparel.

- Chemicals and petrochemicals.
- Food processing.
- Shipping.
- Railways etc.

Services Sectors:

- Information Technology and Information Technology enabled service (IT and IT).
- Tourism and Hospitality services.
- Medical value travel.
- Accounting and finance services.
- Audio visual services.
- Legal services.
- Financial services.
- Education services etc.

Objectives of Make in India program: There are several targets aimed at by the make in India program. They are:

(a) Raising the growth in the manufacturing sector by 12-14% per year.

(b) Creation of 100 million additional jobs in the manufacturing sector by 2022.

(c) Increase the share of the manufacturing sector in the GDP to 25% by 2022.

(d) Skill development among the urban poor and rural migrants to foster inclusive growth.

(e) Enhancing the global competitiveness of the Indian manufacturing sector.

(f) To creates 100 million additional jobs by 2022.

(g) To promote export-led growth.

Key schemes launched to support Make in India program:

(a) Skill India Mission

(b) Start-up India

(c) Digital India

(d) Pradhan Mantri Jan Dhan Yojana (PMJDY)

(e) Smart cities

(f) AMRUT

(g) Swachh Bharat Abhiyan

(h) AGNII

(i) International Solar Alliance (ISA)

Make in India 2.0: Focuses on 27 sectors with a special focus on ten champion sectors including:

Capital goods, auto, defence, pharma, renewable energy, biotechnology, chemicals, leather, textile, and food processing. These ten sectors have the potential to become global champions and drive double-digit growth in manufacturing in the coming years. In the manufacturing sector, the action plans are controlled and coordinated by the Department for Promotion of Industry and Internal Trade (DPIIT).

ATMA NIRBHAR BHARAT

Atma Nirbhar Bharat Abhiyan (self-reliant India mission) is a campaign launched by the central government of India which included Rs 20 lakh crore economic stimulus package and a number of reform proposals.

As part of the relief measures in the aftermath of Covid-19, the prime minister announced a special economic package and gave a clarion call for 'Atma Nirbhar Bharat' or 'self-reliant India'.

He noted that this package totals Rs 20 lakh crore, including the government's recent announcements on supporting key sectors and measured by the Reserve Bank of India, which is equivalent to almost 10% of India's GDP.

The amounts include packages already announced at the beginning of the lockdown incorporating measures from the RBI and the pay-outs under the Pradhan Mantri Garib Kalyan Yojna.

These packages is expected to focus on land, labour, liquidity and laws.

The self-reliant India mission aims towards cutting down import dependence by focusing on substitution which improves safety compliance and quality of goods to gain Global market shares.

Self-reliance neither signifies any exclusionary or isolationists strategies but involves creation of a helping hand to the whole world.

The mission focuses on the importance of promoting 'local' products.

The mission will be carried out in two phases:

Phase 1: It will consider sectors like medical; textile, electronics, plastics and toys where local manufacturing and exports can be promoted.

Phase 2: It will consider products like gems, and jewellery, pharma and steel.

Five pillars of a self-reliant India: To spur growth and to build a self-reliant India Atma Nirbhar Bharat Abhiyan rest on 5 important pillars.

1. **Economy:** Considers a quantum leap rather than an incremental adjustment to turn current difficulty into an advantage.

2. **Infrastructure:** That can be an image of modern India, or it can be the identity of India

3. **Systems:** Driven by 21st century technology and that is not based on old rules.

4. **Democracy:** A vibrant democracy that is the source of energy to make India self-reliant.

5. **Demand:** Where the strength of our demand and supply chain is utilized intelligently.

Salient Features:

Here are the salient features of the Atma Nirbhar Bharat Stimulus package announced by the government of India in May 2020.

- Insurance cover of Rs 50 lakh per health worker.

- 80 crore poor people received 5kg wheat or rice per person for 3 months from May 2020.

- Each household received 1kg of pulses for 3 months from May 2020.

- 20 crore women Jan Dhan account holders received INR 500 per month for 3 months May 2020.

- Free gas cylinders were provided to 8 crore low incomes families for 3 months.

- MNREGA wage was increased to INR 202 a day from INR 182. This benefited 13.62 crore families.

- Front-loaded INR 21000 paid to farmers under PM-Kisan. This benefited 8.7 crore farmers.

- RBI increased the ways means advance limits of states by 60% and the overdraft duration limits.

- The last date for Income tax and GST returns was extended to 30th June 2020.

━━━ CHAPTER-3 ━━━

3.1 INDIA'S CONTRIBUTION TO THE WORLD: MEDICAL SCIENCE– CHARAKA, SUSHRUTA

<u>CHARAKA</u>

Born: Charaka; 1st century C.E.; Ancient India

Known for: Charaka Samhita

Died: 2nd century C.E.

Fields: Medicine

Acharya Charaka: Charaka is the renowned author of the oldest surviving text in Ayurveda, the Charaka Samhita. It is believed that his master or Guru whose name was Punarvasu Atreya, had seven disciples– Agnivesa, Charaka, Bhela, Jatukarna, Parasara, Harita, and Ksharapaani. These seven disciples wrote their own samhita or texts. Agnivesa is said to have had the best version. The revised version of the same is what came to be known as "Charaka Samhita".

Acharya Charaka lived in 100-200 B.C.E. He was one of the fundamental contributors to the ancient art and science of Ayurveda Ayurved a was one of the oldest medical systems based on herbs and its compound raised in the Vedic period of India. Ayurveda means 'lifespan built on knowledge' or 'Science of life' which was practised in India for centuries before the Greek Physician Hippocrates arose

(460-379 B.C.E.). He also authored a book called "Charaka Samhita", which contains eight main chapters. This book has description of 2000 medicines. In the last chapter of Charak samhita there is a one statement that Charak samhita contains 120 adhyayas (chapters) and 12,000 Shlokas.[32] Its contents are divided into 120 chapters in eight specific Sthanas or partitions. They are:

1. Sutra Sthana (30 chapters) - It guides on the core philosophy and beliefs of Ayurveda, and the requisite approach towards treatment.

2. Nidana Sthana (8 chapters) - Gives information about eight primary diseases and their causes.

3. Vimana Sthana (8 chapters) - It gives Ideological advice for practitioners on taste, recommended diet and training.

4. Sharira Sthana (8 chapters) - It gives the explanations of the anatomy of the human body.

5. Indriya Sthana (12 chapters) - Diagnosis and prognosis.

6. Chikitsa Sthana (30 chapters) - Specialized treatment methods.

7. Kalpa Sthana (12 chapters) - It tells us about the methods on how medicines must be prepared for accurate treatment.

8. Siddhi Sthana (12 chapters) - It gives overall health advice.

The final two chapters are attributed to Dridhabala, who is said to have been active around the 4th century C.E.

Charaka also studied the anatomy of the human body and described about 360 bones in the body including teeth. Subsequently, he recognised that the heart is the controlling centre and is connected to the entire body through 13 channels. He also claimed that any obstruction in the main channels led to a disease in the body. Moreover, he was the first physician who started the concept of Digestion, Metabolism and Immunity. Accordingly, he emphasised the body functions based on three Doshas or principles. Those are vata (movement) pitta (transformation) and kapha (lubrication and stability) in a living body. The three Doshas are corresponding to the western classification of humours-wind, bile and phlegm. He further stated that illness is caused due to the imbalance among three energies in the body and the body needs medicine to restore balance. He also prescribed the ethical charter for medical practitioners well prior to the Hippocratic oath.

Eventually, Acharya Charaka stated that "A physician who fails to enter the body of a patient with the lamp of knowledge and understanding, can never treat the disease. He should first study all the factors including environment which influences a patients disease and then prescribe treatment. It is more important to prevent the occurrence of disease than to seek a cure.

SUSHRUTA

Born: 800 B.C., Varanasi

Died: 700 B.C., Kāsī

Parents: Vishvamitra

Books: Sushruta Samhita

Introduction: The great Sushruta is remembered by the world for his contribution to surgery in general and plastic surgery in particular. He wrote one of the world's earliest works on medicine and surgery.

Sushruta (7th or 6th century B.C.E.), an ancient Indian physician and the first surgeon in history, is credited with creating and perfecting surgical techniques. He is also known as the 'father of surgery' and the 'father of plastic surgery'. "Sushruta Samhita", which he wrote on the subject, is regarded as one of the first books ever written on plastic surgery.

Sushruta:

- Sushruta's work concentrates on the application of medical skills rather than providing any information about who he was or where he came from, hence nothing is known about his personal history.

- Since 'Sushruta' is an adjective that means 'famous', not even his birth name is known.

- He might have lived and worked as early as 1000 B.C.E. however, he is typically dated to the 7th or 6th century B.C.E.

- The only thing that is well known for sure about him is that he was a physician who worked near the banks of the Ganges River in Northern India, now Varanasi.

- The "Sushruta Samhita", one of the three books that make up the great trilogy of Ayurvedic medicine, is widely recognised as the earliest literature on cosmetic surgery in existence. The other two are the "Charka Samhita" and "Ashtanga Hridhay".

By the time of Sushruta, surgery was a well-established medical speciality in India, he made major contributions to the development of various surgical procedures and most notably, the invention of aesthetic surgery. His books advise other on precisely how a surgeon should proceed. In the Sushruta Samhita he described in detail the study of anatomy with the aid of a dead body. Sushruta's forte was rhinoplasty (plastic surgery) and ophthalmology (ejection of cataract). Shushruta has described surgery under eight heads, chedya (excision), lakhya (scarification), vedhya (puncturing), esya (exploration), Ahrya (extraction), vsraya (evacuation) and sivya (suturing).[33]

Other contributions by Sushruta:

1. Besides trauma involving general surgery, he gave an in-depth account of the treatment of 12 varieties of fractures and six types of dislocation.

2. Sushruta mentioned the principles of traction, manipulation, apposition, stabilization, and postoperative physiotherapy.

3. He also prescribed measures to induce the growth of lost hair and the removal of unwanted hair.

4. He urged surgeons to achieve perfect healing which is characterized by the absence of any elevation, induration, swelling mass, and the return of normal colouring.

To Sushruta, surgical techniques and instruments were the most valuable of all tantras in medicine because they could produce results almost instantly which made surgery the most important of all medical specialities. Infinite piety, fame, and access to heaven are all available to those who seek it. It extends human life on the planet and aids in the accomplishment of goals and display a respectable level of competencies in daily activities.

3.2 MATHEMATICS ANS ASTRONOMY: ARYABHATTA, BAUDHYANA, BRAHMAGUPTA, RAMANUJAN

ARYABHATTA

Birth: 476 C.E.

Birth Place: Kusumapura, capital Patalipitra in the Gupta Era.

Present Day: Birthplace is known to be Bihar, Patna, India.

Works: His Most Notable work is Aryabhatiya and Arya Siddhanta.

Death: 550 C.E.

Introduction: Aryabhatta was one of the greatest mathematicians and an astronomer from the classical age of Indian mathematics and Indian astronomy. Very little is known of the personal life of Āryabhata, and the summary that follows is based on my essays in Scribner's Encyclopedia of India.[34] He was born in Aśmaka but later lived in Kusumapura, which the commentator Bhāskara I (c. 629) identifies with Pāṭaliputra (modern Patna). It appears that he was the kulapati (head) of the University at Nālandā in Magadha.[35]

Arya Siddhant is the classical work of this greatest scientist. The works of Aryabhatta were of great influence in the Indian sub-continent astronomical tradition and several neighbouring cultures. Not much information is available in history regarding the birth of Aryabhatta. It is believed that Aryabhata was born in 476 C.E. in Kusumapura, Pataliputra (present-day Patna, Bihar). Aryabhata has been the author of several treatises on mathematics and astronomy. The major works of Aryabhatta includes "Aryabhatiya" and "Aryasidhanta". Aryabhatta is a compendium of mathematics and astronomy. The mathematical part of the Aryabhata covers arithmetic, plane trigonometry, algebra, spherical trigonometry, quadratic equations, continued fraction, sums-of-power series and table of sines. His definitions of sine, cosine, versine and inverse sine influenced the birth of trigonometry.

Some scholars have suggested that Āryabhaṭa and other Indian astronomers borrowed certain mathematical techniques and observations from Greek and Babylonian astronomy.[36][37]

Aryabhata's system of astronomy was called the "Aud Ayaka system". Aryabhata also correctly insisted that the earth rotates about its axis daily and that the apparent movement of the stars is a relative motion caused by the rotation of the earth contrary to the then prevailing view the sky rotated. Aryabhatta described the geocentric model of the solar system, in which the sun and moon are each carried by epicycles. They in turn revolve around the earth. Aryabhata also gave a scientific explanation of the solar and lunar eclipses. He reflected sunlight. India's first satellite Aryabhatta and the lunar crater Aryabhatta were named to honour this great Indian scientist. Further, the Aryabhatta Research Institute Observational Sciences (ARIES) as a centre for research and training in astrophysics and astronomy was setup near Nainital (Uttarakhand) in his homeland. Aryabhata's legacy is truly unparalleled, and no one has ever been able to replicate his major achievements at world-class level that are still relevant today. His forward-thinking approach was noteworthy.

The Motion of the Solar System: Aryabhatta suggested that the earth rotates on its axis. According to him the relative movement of the stars is caused by the motion of the earth. In this first chapter of his book Aryabhatiyam, he mentions the number of earth rotations in a yuga. In order to explain this phenomenon, he proposed a geometrical model of the solar system in which the moon and sun were carried by epicycles which means a circle moving on another circle. According to this model, the motion of the planets was governed by two epicycles. The smaller one was slow and the larger one was fast.

Eclipses: Aryabhata explained lunar and solar eclipses with scientific experiments. He stated that all the planets and the moon shine due to the reflected sunlight. He explained the eclipses in terms of shadows falling on the earth.

Death of Aryabhata: Aryabhata, a successful mathematician, astronomer and scientist died at the age of 74. The place and time of death are still unknown. It was believed he spent most of his life in Kusumapura, Pataliputra, the place where he was born.

Conclusion: Aryabhatta truly made the world notice India, in terms of holding scientific knowledge and value that made a difference to the world. He had challenged and contradicted many beliefs that were going on at the time and through calculations provided pieces of evidence for it to be true. The first Indian satellite that was sent to space was named after him as a tribute. We must take pride in his works as Indians.

BAUDHYANA

Birth: 800 B.C.

Death: 740 B.C.

An Indian mathematician named Baudhayana was born around 800 B.C. and passed away in 740 B.C. He was a brahmin priest of the Vedas. He is credited as having created Pythagoras Theorem in its original form. He was the first Indian mathematician to develop several mathematical ideas. One of the mathematicians who applied their knowledge in real-world situations was this skilful artisan. He was the first to compute the value of pi.

Baudhayana (800 B.C.)

- Indian mathematician Baudhayan lived from 800 B.C. till his death in 740 B.C. He was a brahmin priest of Vedas.

- Even before pi was given its official name and the Pythagorean theorem was first used, Baudhayana referred to it.

- At least 1000 years before Pythagoras was born, Baudhyana made the discovery attributed to him.

- He had the ideas for the Pythagoras theorem in his head before the Pythagoras was really created, according to shloka from the Sulba Sutra.

- He wasn't a scribe like Ahmes who just copied documents; neither was he a mathematician in the modern sense.

- He would undoubtedly have had a very high level of education, but he was likely only interested in applying mathematics for his religious beliefs, not for its own sake.

- Unquestionably, Baudhayana composed the Sulba Sutra to provide guidelines for religious ceremonies and it would be seen as practically inevitable that Baudhayana would be a Vedic priest himself.

- The Sulba Sutra's mathematical explanations are included so that altars required for sacrifices can be built precisely.

- The writing makes it obvious that Baudhayana was not only a priest but also a master artisian.

Sulba Sutra: It is a collection of sutra texts used in the Srauta ritual that provides geometry essential for erecting fire altars.

- The Srauta sutras, which are regarded as Vedic appendices, are larger body of literature that includes the Sulba Sutra.

- They are the only source for knowledge about Vedic Indian mathematics. One of a kind Godly gifts were associated with distinctive fire-alter shapes.

- For instance, the Sulba Sutra of Baudhayan is dated to the eighth century B.C.

- Other authors who later produced Sulba Sutra includes Apastamba, Manava, Katyatana, Satyasadha,m Hiranyakesin, Vadhula, Varaha and Kathah, however it is unclear in what order they produced.

The Baudhayana sutras are a group of Vedic Sanskrit texts which covers not only Dharma but also daily rituals, mathematics, etc. They belong to the Taittiriya branch of the Krishna Yajurveda school and are among the earliest texts of the genre.It was compiled in the 8th to 6th centuries B.C.E.

The Baudhayana sutras consist of six texts. They are given below:

1. The Srauta Sutra in 19 Praśnas (questions),

2. The Karmanta Sutra in 20 Adhyayas (chapters),

3. The Dvaidha Sutra in 4 Prasnas,

4. The Grihya Sutra in 4 Prasnas,

5. The Dharma Sutra in 4 Prasnas and

6. The Sulba Sutra in 3 Adhyayas.[38]

Conclusion: Baudhayana was an Indian mathematician who lived from 800 B.C. until roughly 740 B.C. He was a brahmin Vedic priest. The Pythagoras Theorem was first formulated by him. He invented a variety of mathematical concepts as the first Indian mathematician.

BRAHMAGUPTA

Born: 598 C.E. at Bhinmal (Rajasthan, India)

Died: 668 C.E., India

Parents: Jishnugupta

Nationality: Indian

Fields: Astronomy, Mathematics

Early Life:

Brahmagupta was born in 598 C.E. He resided in Bhillamala (Rajasthan,India). Bhillamala was the capital of the Gurjaradesa, West India's second-biggest state, which comprised contemporary India's south side Rajasthan & north side Gujarat. He was always focused to work for finding new concepts.

Brahmagupta (c. 598–c. 668 C.E.) was an Indian mathematician and astronomer. He is the author of two early works on mathematics and astronomy. Indian astronomer and mathematician Brahmagupta lived from 598 to 668 C.E. The "Khandakhadyaka", a more practical text, and the theoretical "Brahmasphutasiddhanta" are two of his early works on mathematics and astronomy. For the first time, Brahmagupta provided guidelines for computing with zero.[39]

Brahmagupta's contribution to Mathematics: The qualities of the zero were established by Brahmagupta, which was critical for the development of mathematics and science. Brahmagupta listed the qualities of zero as follows:

- When we reduce a number from itself, we obtain a zero.

- Any number divided by zero yields a result of zero.

- He found the formula for solving quadratic problems.

- Almost exactly the value of pi (3.162....). He increased the value by 0.66 percent, over the genuine value (3.14).

- He calculated that the earth is closer to the moon than the sun.

- A formula for calculating the area of any four-sided shape whose corners touch the interior of circle was discovered.

- A year is 365 days, 6 hour and 12 minutes and 9 seconds long.

- Brahmagupta mentioned "gravity". "Bodies fall towards the earth because it is a fact that the earth attracts bodies, just as it does in water to flow", he says.

- Brahmagupta invented guidelines for working with positive and negative numbers, including when we add a negative number to a negative number, it is a negative number. Subtracting a negative number from a positive number is equivalent to adding the two numbers.[40]

Contribution to science and astrology: Brahmagupta contended that the earth and the universe are not flat but spherical. He was the first to utilize mathematics to forecast planet locations and lunar and solar eclipse timing. He also computed the duration of the solar year to be 365 days. 5, minute and 19 seconds, which is quite close today's computation of 365 days, 5 hours, and 19 seconds.

Brahmagupta also proposed moved methods to solve quadratic equations that are familiar to current mathematicians. Brahmagupta also researched several higher brain functions of Algebra and Geometry each time expanding on and improving the ancient world's mathematics legally.

RAMANUJAN

Full name: Srinivasa Iyengar Ramanujan

Born: 22 December 1887, Erode

Died: 26 April 1920, Kumbakonam

Srinivasa Ramanujan was an Indian mathematician who made contributions to mathematical analysis and number theory with almost no formal training in pure mathematics. Srinivasa Ramanujan was born on 22 December 1887 in the southern part of India in Tamil Nadu, named Erode. His father Kuppuswamy Srinivasa Lyngen worked as a clerk in a saree shop and his mother, Komalatamma was a housewife. From a very early age, he had a keen interest in mathematics and had already become a child prodigy. He attained his early education and schooling in Madras, where he was enrolled in a local school. His love for mathematics had grown at a very young age and was mostly self-taught. He was a promising student and had won money academic prizes in high school. In 1903 he secured a scholarship to the university of Madras but lost it the following year because he neglected all the other subjects in purest of Mathematics. In 1911 Ramanujan published the first of his paper in the journal of the Indian Mathematical society. In 1903 he began some correspondence with the British mathematician Godfrey H. Hardy which led to a special scholarship from the University of Madras and a grant from Trinity College, Cambridge. In 1918 he was elected to the Royal Society of London. Ramanujan was one of the youngest members of Britain's Royal Society and the first Indian to be elected a fellow of Trinity College, Cambridge University.[41]

Contributions to Mathematics:

Formulas and Equations:

- ➢ Ramanujan compiled around 3,900 results consisting of equations and identities. One of his most treasured findings was his infinite series for pi.

- ➢ He gave several formulas to calculate the digits of pi in many unconventional ways.[42]

Game Theory:

- He discovered a long list of new ideas to solve many challenging mathematical problems, with a significant impetus to the development of game theory.

- His contribution to game theory is purely based on inflation and natural talent and remains unrivalled to this day.[43]

Ramanujan Books:

- One of Ramanujan's notebooks was discovered by George Andrews in 1976 in the library at trinity college. Later the contents of these notebooks were published as a book.

Ramanujan Number:

- 1729 is known as the Ramanujan number.

- It is the smallest number which can be expressed as the sum of two different cubes in two different ways.

- 1729 is the sum of the cubes of 10 and 9 cube of 10 is 1000 and cube of 9 is 729 adding the two numbers of results in 1729.

Others contributions: Ramanujan's other notable contributions include hypergeometric series, the Riemann series, the elliptic integrals, mock theta function, theory of divergent series, and the functioned equation of the zeta function.

3.3 PHYSICS: KANAD, P.C. RAY, RAMAN

KANAD

Born: Gujarat; 6th – 2nd century B.C.E.

Region: Indian philosophy

School: Vaisheshika

Main interests: Metaphysics

Ethics: Physics

Notable ideas: Atomism

Full name: Kanada

Kanad was born in 600 B.C. in Dwarka, Gujarat. His real name was Kashyap. He was the son of philosopher named Ulka. Since his childhood days he displayed a keen sense of service. Minute things attracted his attention. Kanad was the first person in the world to discuss atoms and molecules. He was the first person who propounded that the parmanu (Atoms) was an indestructive particle of matter. According to him, the material universe is made up of parmanu (Atoms). When matter is divided and subdivided, we reach a stage beyond which no division is possible, the invisible element of matter is parmanu (Atoms). Kanad explained that this invisible, indestructible atom cannot be sensed through any human organ. This theory occurred to him while kanad was walking with food in his hands, breaking it into small pieces when he realised that he was unable to divide the food into any further parts, it was too small. From this movement Kanad conceptualized the idea of a particle that could not be divided any further. He called the invisible matter parmanu (Atoms). Kanad further held that atoms of a same substance combined with each other to produce dvyanuka (bioatomic molecules) and tryanuka (triatomic molecules). Kanad also put forward the idea that atoms could be combined in various ways to produce chemical changes in presence of other factors such as heat.

 UNDERSTANDING HISTORY

Kanad founded the Vaisheshika school of philosophy where he taught his ideas about the atom and the nature of universe. He wrote a book on his research "Vaisheshika Darsham". People started calling him 'Acharya' which means teacher and became known as 'The father of Atomic Theory.'

He described the universe with six categories, which are dravya, which is defined as a substance. Guna, which is defined as quality. Karman, which is defined as motion. Samanya, which is defined as generic species. Visesa, which is defined as unique trait and Samavaya, is defined as inherence.

Conclusion: Thus, the great philosophers and saints like Sage Kanad were parallelly able to travel on both philosophy and spirituality. He has made several people think about science. He was a great inspiration for several other philosophers and thinkers too.

PRAFULLA CHANDRA RAY

Date of birth: August 2, 1861

Date of death: June 16, 1944

Born: Khulna, Bangladesh

Early Life and Education:

Prafulla Chandra Ray is one of the most famous scientists that India has ever produced P.C. Ray was an eminent Indian chemist, educationist, historian, industrialist and philanthropist. He established the first modern Indian research school in chemistry. He is regarded as the father of chemical science in India. He was born on 2nd August, 1861 at Khulna (now Bangladesh). He started his primary education in a village school. Later, he got his education in some schools like Hare School and Albert School. After that he passed the entrance examination in 1879.[44]

He was known as the 'Father of Indian Chemistry'. Prafulla Chandra Roy was a well-known Indian scientist and teacher who established Bengal Chemical and Pharmaceutical Works Ltd., India's first pharmaceutical company in 1901.

He was also a very passionate and devoted social worker; he did not support the caste system. His father, Harish Chandra Roy was a landlord who loved learning and he built up an extensive library in his home. His mother Bhubanmohini Devi was well-educated with liberal views. The family moved to Kolkata when Prafulla was nine years old and he attended the Hare School. Unfortunately, Prafulla fell ill and returned to village in 1874. It took two years for Prafulla to recover and he was permanently frail with digestive issues and insomnia. During his recovery he enjoyed reading in his father's well equipped library. He returned to Kolkata and attended Albert School and in 1879 and, after passing the entrance exam, began studies at the Metropolitan College (now Vidyasagar College). Prafulla also studied chemistry at the presidency college this soon became his favourite subject, he built a laboratory at home and began experimenting. In 1882, Prafulla won a scholarship to Edinburgh University, UK and he gained his degree there in 1885. Remaining at Edinburgh to undertake research, he was awarded a D.sc. in 1887 and the " Hope Prize" for his thesis on "Conjugated sulphates of the Copper-Magnesium, Group of Isomorphous Mixture and Molecules combinations". He breathed his last breath on June 16th, 1944.

Contributions and Achievements: Prafulla Roy returned to Calcutta in 1889 and became a professor of chemistry at the Presidency College in Calcutta in 1889. He established a research laboratory and slowly gathered a group of dedicated students who researched with him. He published around 150 research papers during his life time. Many of his articles on science were published in renowned journals of his time. His research include the discovery of the stable compound mercurous nitrate in 1896. While studying nitrite and hyponitrite compounds and their compounds. He also researched organic compounds containing sulphur, double salts, homomorphism and fluorination. In 1892 with a small capital of 700 INR, he established Bengal Chemical works. It flourished under his management. The company initially produced herbal products and indigenous medicines. In 1901, the enterprise became a limited company, Bengal Chemical and Pharmaceutical Works Ltd. (BCPW) and it is first Indian Pharmaceutical company. Gradually the company expands and became a leading chemical and medicine producers. Prafulla Roy was interested in ancient texts and after much research published "The History of Hindu Chemistry" in two volumes in 1902 and 1908. The work detailed the extensive knowledge of metallurgy and medicines in ancient India. In 1916, Prafulla Roy retired from President College and joined Calcutta University where he worked for more than 20 years. He represented many Indians universities at international seminars and conferences. He was elected as the Indian Science Congress President in 1920. His autobiography "Life and Experiences of a Bengali Chemist", published in two volumes in 1932 and 1935 documents of his own. Remaining a bachelor throughout his life, Prafulla Roy retired becoming professor Emeritus in 1936 aged 75. He died on 16 June aged 82.[45]

Conclusion: He was a very inspiring teacher. He dedicated his spare time in research. He published his works on Ayurveda -'The History of Hindu Chemistry'. Acharya P. C. Roy was a great patriot. He was highly influenced by leaders like S. N. Banerjee and Mahatma Gandhi. He loved his fellow men and devoted himself to the relief works during the calamities. Acharya Prafulla Chandra Roy dedicated himself to the cause of spreading scientific knowledge among the mass.

C.V. RAMAN

Born: 7 November 1888, Tiruchirappalli

Died: 21 November 1970, Bengaluru

Full name: Chandrasekhara Venkata Raman

Children: Venkatraman Radhakrishnan, Chandrasekhar Raman

Parents: R. Chandrasekhar Iyer, Parvathi Ammal

Chandrasekhara Venkata Raman was an Indian physicist known mainly for his work in the field of light scattering which is known as the "Raman Effect". His work was influential in the growth of science in India. He was the recipient of the Noble prize for Physics in 1930 for the discovery of light scattering phenomena now known as "Raman Scattering". He was the first Asian to receive a Noble prize in any branch of Science.[46]

Early life: Raman was born on 7 November, 1888 in Tirucirapalli, Madras Presidency to Tamil parents. He completed his secondary and higher secondary education at the age of 11 and 13. He topped his Bachelor's degree at the University of Madras with honours in Physics from Presidency College at the age of 13. He published his first research paper at the age of 18 while he still was a graduate student. He completed his M.A. degree at the age of 19. He joined Indian Financial Service in Calcutta as Assistant Accountant General at the age of 19 as his father wanted him to join financial service. In Calcutta, he got acquainted with the Indian Association for Cultivation Science (IACS), which allowed him independent research. He married Lokasundari Ammal in 1907.[47]

Scientific Career: In 1917, he got the opportunity to join university as the professor of Physics. He also became the permanent visiting professor at B.H.U. He was elected as Fellow of the Royal Society in 1924. In 1926, he established the Indian Journal of Physics as the first editor. On 28 Feb. 1928, Raman led an experiment with K.S. Krishna, on the scattering of light, when he discovered, what is called Raman Effect. It gave further proof of the quantum nature of light. Raman spectroscopy a new field was come to be based on this phenomenon after Raman Effect. In 1933, he left Kolkata to join the Indian Institute of Science in Bangalore as its first Indian Director which was started by donations of Maharaja of Mysore, Nizam of Hyderabad and Jamshed ji Tata. He founded the Indian Academy of Science in 1934 and started publishing the proceedings of the Academy. In 1943, he started a company called Travancore Chemical and Manufacturing Co. Ltd. which manufactured Potassium Chlorate for the Match Industry. In 1947, he became the first National Professor in the new government of independent India. He retired from IISC in 1948 and established the Raman Research Institute in Bangalore in 1949. He was against the control of research programmes by the govt. such as the establishment of Bhabha Atomic Research Centre (BARC), Defence Research and Development Organisation (DRDO) and the Council of Scientific and Industrial Research (CSIR).

He remained hostile of the people associated with these institutions such as Homi Bhabha, S.S Bhatnagar. He died in October in 1970 after cardiac arrest.[48]

C.V. Raman's Contribution as an Author: C.V. Raman's discoveries led him to write a set of books which are listed below:

Vol. 1: Scattering of Light (Ed. S Ramaseshan)

Vol. 2: Acoustic

Vol. 3: Optica

Vol. 4: Optics of Minerals and Diamond

Vol. 5: Physics of Crystals

Vol. 6: Floral Colours and Visual Perception

Conclusion: C.V. Raman was very disciplined and hardworking. His determination was very high. His life inspired many and will inspire everyone who is deprived of facilities. His alternative line of thinking and imagining differently made him famous. Thus, we can say that the life of this great personality is valid proof that one can do miracles even if he/she is not rich or does not have any good facilities.

BIBLIOGRAPHY

1. Raychaudhuri, Hemchandra. Studies in Indian Antiquities. Calcutta: University of Calcutta, 1989.

2. Singh, U. (2009). A History of ancient and early medieval India: from the Stone Age to the 12th century (PB). Pearson Education India.

3. Yumol, E. P. (2015). Perception Of Entrepreneurs on The Effect Of Tourism On The Socio-Economic Development of Tabuk City, Kalinga. Kasc Research Journal, 151.

4. Sengupta, S. Rewinding the Ancient past: Social condition during Mauryan Empire. International Journal of Humanities & Social Science Studies, 3, 257-264.

5. Bhat, R. M. (2022). An Analytical Study of the Kushan Rule in Kashmir. Journal of Psychology and Political Science (JPPS) ISSN, 2799-1024.

6. G.J. Toomer, The chord table of Hipparchus and early history of Greek trigonometry. Centaurus, vol. 18, pp. 6-28, 1973.

7. Pingree, The recovery of early Greek astronomy from India. Journal of History of Astronomy, vol. 7, pp. 109-123, 1976.

8. Loeschner, H. (2012). Kanishka in Context with the Historical Buddha and Kushan Chronology. Glory of the Kushans–Recent Discoveries and Interpretations, 137-194.

9. Mookerji, R. (1989). The Gupta Empire. Motilal Banarsidass Publ..

10. Bornberg, R. (2023). India: Some Insights. In Urban India: Cultural Heritage, Past and Present (pp. 21-48). Cham: Springer International Publishing.

UNDERSTANDING HISTORY

11. Chakrabarti, D. K., & Lal, M. Political History and Administration.

12. Venkataraman, T. K. (1960). South India and Indian Culture. Early Period. Cahiers d'Histoire Mondiale. Journal of World History. Cuadernos de Historia Mundial, 6(1), 331.

13. Rao, M. R., & Rao, M. R. (1959, January). THE HOME OF THE PALLAVAS. In Proceedings of the Indian History Congress (Vol. 22, pp. 67-72). Indian History Congress.

14. Francis, E. (2021). Pallavas. The Encyclopedia of Ancient History: Asia and Africa, 1-4.

15. Ramesh, S., & Ramesh, S. (2018). The Chola Dynasty: 350 BC to 1279 AD. The Rise of Empires: The Political Economy of Innovation, 171-199.

16. Baby, K. (2024). Art And Architecture Under Imperial Cholas-A Study. Migration Letters, 21(S7), 17-21.

17. Palat, R. A. (1986). Popular revolts and the state in Medieval South India: A study of the Vijayanagara empire (1360-1565). Bijdragen tot de Taal-, Land-en Volkenkunde, (1ste Afl), 128-144.

18. Madan, T. N. (1989). Religion in India. Daedalus, 114-146.

19. Sharma, S. K. (2002). Life Profile & Biography of Buddha. Diamond Pocket Books (P) Ltd..

20. Ahan, A. A. (2023). Sufi and Bhakti Tradition: Corresponding and Divergent Trends. In Islam in India (pp. 31-39). Routledge.

21. Kumar, S. V. Raja Ram Mohan Roy–A Great Reformer–Analysis.

22. Kvamme, K. L. (1992). A predictive site location model on the High Plains: An example with an independent test. Plains Anthropologist, 37(138), 19-40.

23. Sanjay Singh Gaharwar, op.cit, p.256.

24. Luniya.B.N., op.cit, p.488.

25. V. D Savarkar described the Revolt of 1857 as First War of Independence.

26. Sharma, H. D. 100 Best Letters 1847-1947, Harper Collins Publishers India, Delhi, 2000, p.14

27. Eric Strokes, Cristopher and Alan balayl, The peasant armed: the Indian revolt of 1857, (1986, 3rd Edition), 221

28. Ibid

29. Rudrangshu Mukherjee, Awadh in Revolt, 1857-1858: A Study of Popular Resistance, 2002 1st Edition, 196

30. Pratap Singh Mukharya, The Revolt of 1857: Saugor and Nerbudda Territories, 2001 1st edition, 120

31. Supra1 Parliamentary Papers, 1860, III, Foreign Department, No. 257, Camp Kanpur, 4 Nov1859. Jeffery, Amen.

32. Op.cit, p. 15.

33. Bhattacharya, S. (2009). Sushrutha-our proud heritage. Indian Journal of Plastic Surgery, 42(02), 223-225.

34. Charak Samhita, with Charaka Chandrika Hindi commentary, by Dr. Brahmanand Tripathi and Dr. Ganga Sahay Pandey, Siddhi Sthana Chapter 12, Verse No. 34.

35. Chaukhamba Surbharti Prakashan, 2007.p.1341.

36. S. Kak, Aryabhata and Aryabhatiya. Essays in Encyclopedia of India (edited by Stanley Wolpert). Charles Scribner's Sons/Gale, New York, 2005.

37. K.S. Shukla and D.V. Sarma, Āryabhatīya of Āryabhata. Indian National Science Academy, 1976.

38. Kulikov, L. (2004). The Baudhāyana Śrautasūtra, critically edited and translated by CG Kashikar. Acta Orientalia Vilnensia, 5, 281-285.

39. Bhattacharyya, R. K. (2011). Brahmagupta: the ancient Indian mathematician. Ancient Indian Leaps into Mathematics, 185-192.

   UNDERSTANDING HISTORY

40. SHIVAKUMAR, D. On the History of Indian Mathematics.

41. Berndt, B. C., & Rankin, R. A. (2000). The books studied by Ramanujan in India. The American Mathematical Monthly, 107(7), 595-601.

42. Murty, M. R., & Murty, V. K. (2013). The mathematical legacy of Srinivasa Ramanujan (p. 15). New Delhi: Springer.

43. Ramanujan, R. (2021). Variable-Player Learning for Simulation-Based Games Madelyn Gatchel (Doctoral dissertation, Davidson College).

44. Hazra, Kalyan; Kumar, Deepak; Dutta, Sreya; Mangal, Anupam K; Babu, Gajji. Life and works of Acharya Prafulla Chandra Ray: A man with ultra luminosity. Journal of Research in Ayurvedic Sciences 8(Suppl 1):p S105-S109, May 2024. | DOI: 10.4103/jras.jras_300_23

45. Ray, P. C. (2022). Acharya Prafulla Chandra Ray: A Revisit to his life and work. science and culture.

46. Parameswaran, U. (2011). CV Raman: a biography. Penguin Books India.

47. Singh, R. (2002). CV Raman and the Discovery of the Raman Effect. Physics in Perspective, 4, 399-420.

48. Jayaraman, A., & Ramdas, A. K. (1988). Chandrasekhara Venkata Raman. Physics Today, 41(8), 56-64.

"Never put efforts to prove your intelligence,
let time disclose your identity."

Dr. Adil Firdous Wani

Name: Dr. Adil Firdous Wani

Born Date: 21st March1993

Contact No: 9596760436

Creative Work:

- Published a research paper titled "A study of Buddhist art of the Lower Krishna Valley" in AIRO International Journal in Vol XIII, January 2018

- Published a research paper titled "A study of Premature Image of the Buddhist and Krishna Valley" in AIRO International Journal in Vol XVI, May 2018

- Published an article titled "The Insurrection of1857 in British India: The First war of Independence" in Journal of Emerging Technologies and Innovative Research in Vol6 Issue 5, May 2019.

- Published an article titled "Mahmud Ghazni, the Pillager ofenormous wealth from India" in the International Journal of Scientific Research and Engineering Development in Vol3 Issue 1-Jan-Feb.2020.

- Presented a Research Paper orally on the topic "Historical Medicinal Plants of Jammu and Kashmir" in two days International Conference on 25-26 November 2022.

Professional Work:

- Worked as a Teaching Assistant in Higher Education Department in 2015 and 2016 at Government Degree College Bhaderwah, District Doda, Jammu and Kashmir.

- Worked as a Teaching Assistant in Higher Education Department in 2017 at Government Degree College Bani, District Kathua, Jammu and Kashmir.

- Worked as a Lecturer in Higher Education Department in 2022-2023 at Government Degree College Billawar, District Kathua, Jammu and Kashmir.

- Worked as a Lecturer in Higher Education Department in 2023-2024 at Government Degree College Doda, District Doda, Jammu and Kashmir.

- Presently working as a Lecturer in Higher Education Department at Govt. Degree College Bhaderwah, District Doda, Jammu and Kashmir.